I'm FREE, I'm Free, I'm Free:

NOW WHAT?

A SEMISERIOUS
Guide to Early Housekeeping or
Things You Wouldn't Let Your Family Tell You

Janet McCart

"Being human is hard, and it takes a long time."

PC | PUBLICATION
CONSULTANTS
WE BELIEVE IN THE POWER OF AUTHORS

PO Box 221974 Anchorage, Alaska 99522-1974
books@publicationconsultants.com—www.publicationconsultants.com

ISBN 978-1-59433-481-8
eBook ISBN 978-1-59433-482-5
Library of Congress Catalog Card Number: 2014942469

Manufactured in the United States of America.

I rise in the morning
Torn between a desire
To improve the world and
A desire to enjoy
The world. This makes it
Hard to plan a day.

E. B. White

Table of Kind-Of Contents

Seriously, but not too seriously,
what you can expect to be painful

You Are Adrift

First question

How does a quarter-cup of sticky, colored liquid, (perhaps wine), splash out, and explore six feet in every direction? How can it stain and stick to things that aren't even in the room?

This system of things called life has upset your balance, maybe even caused you to question your sanity. Think about it. (But, don't get stuck in mind-mud. *You know what I mean.*)

Housekeeping Gets A Bad Rap

Housekeeping is mysterious. Yes. Really. It is an area that will test your belief about reality, about what *can* or *can't* happen, here on planet earth. For example: *Peanut butter toast will always fall jelly-side down.* Your 'confidence' shirt will always have a spot when you need it. See, mysterious.

No younger person wants to talk about housekeeping, laundry, or living on the clean side. It is the opposite of sexy and dating. It's a chore. It won't go away.

We are here today, to break-up the mental barriers that cause you to think *you are allergic to cleaning*. No such allergy exists. Sorry.

The truth about cleanness and sexiness and dating

The first clue: Vehicle[1]. Does the *possible attraction's* car look like it could belong to the homeless? A car full of newspapers, clothes, shoes, rotten smells, greasy tools, car parts, and bags or clothes is your first warning sign of what is to come. This person doesn't do *clean*. If you *don't either*, it's a match made for a little while.

A guy or a gal who is semi-serious about a person should hear alarm bells if he/she walks into one's place which is so cluttered that there is nowhere to sit. Kitchen counters overrun with crumbs and bike tires, a roach rambling about, and laundry on the dining table—these things don't say *welcome*.

9 repeat: if the other person prefers the opposite of your preference, if they are *clean* to your *messy*, no matter how *hot*— — hot can go cold—walk away. Nothing good can come of this. *See "Law of You Can't Change People" on page 40.* Nearly every

---

1   Please do not use those tree "fresheners" that hang from your mirror. They can kick off an asthma or allergy attack so fast you'll be madly scrubbing away at your upholstery trying to remove another least-liked icky substance.

woman *believes* it is possible to change someone. I could write a book. I did. We'll talk more about this later.

I don't want to cause you existential angst at such a sensitive time in your life. But it is so: **everything on the planet bows to the physical laws of the universe.** The universe! Physics! How could your little divot of life be so compromised by earthly physical laws? It bends the mind.

You may say, "I don't know anything about physics and I don't want to." However, you already have a pretty good handle on it. You just didn't know what to call it. Think of these common examples which you have probably tested out:

✓ You put your bowl of Jello/yogurt/ice cream/soup on the edge of your kitchen counter, you turn around and hear it hit and explode on the floor. (And you'll do that again just to test whether the *gravity switch* is always on.)

✓ Irritable about being forced to do such lowly labor as raking, you go and stomp on the prongs of the rake in order to reach the handle because you don't want to bend over, and handle pops up and hits you between the eyes. (This is embarrassing, weird, and you never do that again.)

✓ You put your drink on the dash of your car for just a second. You touch the brake, and put into motion a vehicle baptizing with sticky fluid. It can even end up in your hair. From now on you use the cup holder. (Or, not. Some people are slower than others.)

✓ **The classic,** you have your cup of coffee (or whatever) and go the sit at the table. You reach for the newspaper and bump your coffee. You look at the cup—only about a quarter of it splashed out. Yet, that quarter splashes on your sleeve, the place mat, the table, your lap, the chair seat, and to the floor with plenty to spare. It's impossible! How could a quarter cup go so far?

We are venturing into the realm of 'you won't believe it' and 'you can't win.' The laws don't care. However, you will feel the need to test each one, more than once. Oh, well.

The Law of Gravity dictates

In your own place you pick-up after yourself, or live like a hoarder, or have a great roommate, or hire someone to do it for you. (Problems, *See "Joys of Roommates" on page 39.*)

What we **know** is there are **no** exceptions to the Physical rules of the Universe. I repeat, no exceptions, not even for you. Picture

Reader danger, fair warning:

A note for sticklers and Critic's Club devotees: you won't like this book, and you don't need this book. But, you might want to read about those wild and crazy folk who walk on the other side. Let me be clear. *I'm not seeking critical feedback.* This book is not perfect, but it's my book. You have the freedom to write your own. A seven year old will be handling my messages..

Law of Ideas

No good idea ever gets properly implemented.

J. McCart

Example:

Murphy's Law as applied to housekeeping is painfully perfect. What can go wrong will go wrong—at the worst time. Without fail.

Observe advice from wise King Solomon

"When anyone is replying to a matter before he/she hears it, that is foolishness on his/her part."

PROV. 18:13

a heavily armored tank. Now picture baby-bumper cars. Who's gonna move who?

Life will be gentler if you make your peace with these laws. Why? That's the way God made it. And, if you don't believe in a creator, you will soon believe in Murphy and his laws.

What You Can and Can't Expect

In the following text you will be made aware of many of **Murphy's Laws**, and **Life Laws and Rules**. Some of these rules are not written down. They are the worst. And that's where we're going.

Onward, adventurous people, to progress in our business.

> **Monologue:** a long speech monopolizing conversation—or—you can talk but I can't hear you.

> **Think:** a different way of seeing and incorporating things you didn't see before.

This book is not normal. It's more of a friendly *monologue* that introduces you to household and life experiences that will come your way. We'll try to cover questions you hadn't yet thought to ask. This book is for those who have been reluctant to implement the idea of *bending down and picking it up*. And, for those who have put off using their manners, and it's starting to be a problem.

Physical Laws, Life Truths, and Living On Your Own

This is life and death and the popcorn in between.

Household (your household): *Focus of one's domestic attention*—social unit setting, abode, domicile, congenial environment, apartment, condo, house, room, nest.

The Universe sets the only laws that are not breakable. They do appear to bend sometimes. But that's just smoke and mirrors. These laws don't accept excuses, and they don't break.

Still, **you** are part of the universe! We will look at these laws as they apply to you, your life, and your household!

This book offers suggestions on how you may survive and take care of yourself, and your home space on the first try, or the second. We're only shooting for "try" here. Go see Martha if you want "perfect."

Relax. There is absolutely no chance that you will not screw up something. So, you may as well have a sense of humor. Kick back and take in the best kind of wisdom, that hard-won wisdom that comes from the painful experiences of others.

It's time to organize and clean, and to clean and organize. For the rest of your life. Dust never stops dusting. Sticky things never stop sticking. Clothes never pick themselves up. The refrigerator never cleans itself. Neither does the toilet.—I know, bad news. But we'll assume that the Martha followers have drifted away. So you might want to follow the motto:

You can't do it all wrong,
and you can't do it all right, so just do it.

Sir Isaac Newton's **Law of Gravity** says: what goes up must come down. That's the iceberg tip of physics. We combine that law with a preference for a **cleanish** home, and that means picking up after yourself, or hiring someone else to do so. (If you can afford it, it's a fine way to go.)

It's the little things that break you down.

Life is easier if you take your shoes/boots off at the door, put your trash in the trash, put cold groceries in the refrigerator, have a place to put your bag, and hang up your clothes.—But it seems so much more appealing to do it later. Except that later, as you sit in a pile of shoes, coats, bags, and potato chips, it's not so appealing.

So this is personal. For your own safety, you need to know the rules. Try to get into the spirit of the this game of life.

Boo Yah!

"Gravity is reality"

Sometimes it really hurts our feelings when nature's **Physical Laws** are indifferent to us, or even seem to be attacking us. **WHY ME?!** We cry as the birthday cake topples and skids across the back seat. **WHY ME?!** You'll cry as you are kicked off the airplane by security folk because you are crying about how much you lost in Vegas.

Some of these laws come with rights' of passage and have been tested for millennia. Some directives are the basis for our golden rule language, the tried and true laws that come from the Bible, science and from Roman philosophers really don't vary much.

Backyard philosophers have a lot of strange experiences under their hats. Often they are a comfort to talk to. Most of them have graduated from the University of Hard Knocks. Some are still taking classes.

You will take classes too. Some *Knockers* have an advantage. They will actually learn from other people's experiences. In other words, you can experience hard knocks, all sorts of physical and mental pain directly, or learn pain free from a distance *if* you are able to listen and apply what you learn. *If* you choose to stay in hard knocks (HN) school, this book is probably not for you.

Notice the last paragraph contains the words, you can. It does not say, you must. You may be lathered up about inventing your own university of experience. When you're done you will want to share your pain with others too. So you might want to write your own book.

Relax

There is something reassuring about these no-give-ever laws. You don't have to wonder what is going to happen. They are absolute. However, you are probably not used to thinking of laws as absolute.

> "I don't think that word means what you think it means."
>
> Movie: Princess Bride

Let's review these initial worldly definitions as we prepare to be educated beyond your wildest dreams. Yes, words are cool.

> **Law:** A recognized custom or practice whose violation must or should result in penalty, injury, loss, or pain; the word "Law" is often capitalized when revealing the will of God as set forth in the Bible.

Rules: the exercise of authority or control; a
prescribed guide for conduct or action.

Disease: disease as it applies to humans includes a
medical condition with symptoms; or as it applies
to society: a harmful development as in icky social
situation and institutional scenes.

Germs: a small mass of living substance capable of
developing into an organism or one of its parts;
something that initiates development, and is
generally mushy and not good to smell or eat or
wipe around.

Legal terms that will be used in your every-day future. See,
you don't even have to have a law degree?

Caveat: warning or proviso, something said as
a warning, caution, or qualification (I will sell
this to you with the caveat that you will deliver
it by Monday).

Caveat emptor: the commercial principle that the
buyer is responsible for making sure that goods
bought are of a reasonable quality (or the
FAMED: Let the BUYER BEWARE).

Precedent: an action or decision, generally a legal
one, that can be subsequently used as an example
for similar decisions, or to justify a similar action.

Precedent is a tricky one. Say *yes* once, and you could commit
yourself to further *yeses* in similar situations.

Say a box store pays a settlement to someone who was standing in their shopping cart, dancing, and fell. Legally, they've set a precedent that they will pay for such thing, leading the way in similar law suits. We've come to a place in litigation that can be like mud, and the next person to dance in a cart, can get hurt, and be paid a settlement. (This is why businesses fight so these nonsense lawsuits so hard.)

Consider how precedent could link to lending money, doing someone else's work, taking office supplies from work, drinking, smoking, sex… well you get the idea. *Beware of setting precedents.*

> **Mitigation:** This is basically a deal (set up) that says—If I clean up this mess, I will be forgiven for the other worse mess that I made. It is useful for getting back into someone's good graces after one blows it.

● ●

Murphy's Law(s) *Brilliant but Painful*

Anything that can go wrong, will go wrong, and at the worst possible time. No kidding.

● ●

The Big One

You would have to have been living in a box to not have heard of **Murphy's Law**. If so, get out of the box! This Law is already

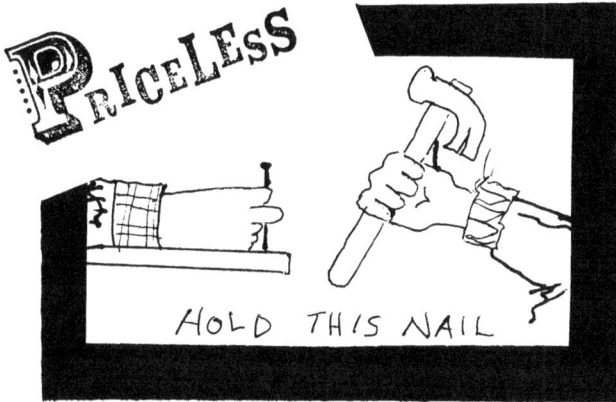

PRICELESS

HOLD THIS NAIL

active, kicking your posterior, and taking names in your life. (You may not have noticed.) Remember the peanut butter toast? Remember the flying soda? Remember the suspicious spots on your new and favorite shirt? Did you imagine these things would happen the first time? Remember being 'late' for an important appointment? Do you recall the stuff that hurt? People who read you like a primer? Do you remember when your romantic other overheard you talking about how good so-and-so looked?

These are not accidents.

It's better if you simply accept this law to be true. However, you, like most people—you will hang on to the belief that all the stupid things have 50/50 odds, and at some point they will swing in your favor.

Well, a broken clock is right twice a day.

50/50 {not}

But, **Murphy's Law** has pushed its way into our little bit of reality like an octopus embracing a pile of fish. Murphy shows us how the odds are tipped by *us*, ruining the 50/50 theory. Humans tend to work toward things that could go wrong more often than things that could go right. And, we're good at it. An unpleasant description of this trait could be called: willful, self-destructive, not very smart, or overempowered.

Add tension, anxiety, deadlines, dates, fear, and other such irritations, and some form of **Murphy's Law** will come up and poke you in the eye. When things happen that you have sworn would never happen to you, it is bewildering. It will rock your view of the world. Hello! Murphy's here!

If you have managed your expectations in that you know this is not a perfect place, and you can't make it be perfect—then you won't be so surprised or angry at the road bumps—you'll just be moderately surprised and angry. But the song says: you've gotta have hope, miles and miles and miles of hope. I'm not promising anything.

When you make toast with jelly for breakfast, and you eat it on the run, because you're late, the toast and jelly will slide off your plate/napkin, skip off your shirt, and land jelly side down on the floor—you won't think it is funny. You would be a marvelous person if you did.

Another classic: (this example gets to be male) He gets to fly to a special event on the company's dime. This is a big deal. However he didn't set his alarm clock. He is late. The clothing he planned to wear seems to have developed spots overnight. So, he changes clothes, and swills down a cup of yogurt as he heads out the door. The yogurt will escape the spoon and cup and drip down the front of his shirt. He dabs away with fast food napkins (see Wipes) that turn into little white balls on the fabric of your shirt.

You've just entered the out-of-sync-twilight-zone.

Law of Out-of-Sync

Oh, Well ...

Law of Out-of-Sync

You can't prove anything, but somehow you got *a bubble off level.* The world tipped. And it's getting stranger as the minutes tick by.

* *

What isn't working for you isn't working

Our volunteer guy is now officially **out of sync** with the universe. Yet he presses on. He might even remain hopeful. In his car he starts to sweat from head to toe. However, every traffic light, slow driver, or piece of heavy equipment seems to have lined up for him. He finally gets to the airport and can't find a parking spot.

He bounces up and down and sweats through the airport security line where progress is frog-speed (forward, backward, and sideways). He runs to his gate, and watches his plane push back.—It is very hard to clamp down on expletive deletes as security takes him by the arm for acting crazed.

This is classic **Law of Out-of-Sync**, working hand in hand with **Murphy's Law**.

You are beginning to see the ghostly Law of Out-of-Sync. You wonder if it could sneak up on you. Maybe it already has and you didn't recognize it.

If you can, just stop. All this pressure is backing up on you, but instead of pressing harder, you must force yourself to stop. In this situation you can't go forward by pushing forward. To get yourself back in sync, have a cup of your favorite beverage, sit down, and breathe. The start of your day proved you weren't going to get anything done anyway. Some of you will be able to go home and go back to bed. But the laws are rarely so kind as to allow that.

Let's go see what other trouble we can get into.

Laws and Rules that Should Scare You

Law of Space Relations

No empty cupboard or closet or drawer or hall or room or deck or porch will remain unfilled. *(Unless you happen to be with the CIA.)*

• •

Another aspect of **Murphy's Laws is the Law of Space Relations**. (Not relatives from space.)

Your belongings will rapidly expand to overrun all available space. Some of your belongings will multiply, especially the fuzzy food and bathroom blobs. Plastic lids and tee shirts multiply, and they will not match anything. You'll never have the right number of hangars or chairs or side tables. Mail will stack up remorselessly. That is unless you are with Homeland security. Spies don't have junk.—Hey, it's a job.

This law can be countered by self-discipline.

Bring/buy one thing home, and get rid of one thing.

The idea is sterling. Application takes discipline. Discipline it is. So you put the unusable things in the trash, and recyclable things in boxes and bags by the door, or in the trunk of your car. Warning: you will think you can stop here. It's a trick.

Your recycle stuff will likely sit there looking ugly for months. It's hard to follow through with those last 2 minutes, and get to the drop box. Do it. Swing by the drop box of your nearest thrift shop. You won't believe how good it feels to get that stuff out of your life.

On top of the **Law of Attraction** and the **Law of Missing Things** contribute to the **Law of Out-of-Sync**. The **Law of Missing Things** is another paranormal law. It's hard to prove, and hard to deny. Keys, important papers, money, a sock, a shoe, a password, a pen, a jack-knife, a ring, medications, and on and on. You begin to see. The older you get, the worse it gets. Multi-tasking aggravates the syndrome dramatically. The down side is that the paranormal enjoy your frenzy and irritation. Sorry, I have no help for you here.

● ●

Murphy's Law of Moving

Moving is an activity that causes friends and family to disappear from the grid.

● ●

This is a tough law. You need to do *some* preparation for moving, or there will not be a rental truck left in town. So, your stuff will be flying out of the back of your friend's pickup or hatchback, and braiding itself into the weeds on the side of the road.

You always wondered who lost their stuff that way. (How could a person not know they lost a king-size mattress? All the cushions to the couch?)

Plan on it to be raining hard, or snowing hard, or be hotter than 100 degrees. Some of this **could and should** have been planned in the face of **Murphy's Law**. **Murphy's Law** proves there are so many ways moving can go wrong. *See "Moving" on page 51.*

• •

Law of Diminished Returns or The Law of There is no Free Lunch

Nothing is free. (Get over it.) As a rule, a free gain is not worth the free pain.

• •

A little "Diminished" story

An acquaintance asks you along, and gives you his/her extra ticket for front-row blow-out concert. Your friend wants to drive. As you hit the road you realize you made the first mistake. The acquaintance drives like a crazy person (only not as well). Once inside he/she proceeds to bounce off the concert facility walls, bumps into scary people, borrows your phone, and leaves the concert without telling you. That is **Diminished Returns** with a sprinkle of **Murphy**.

The big lesson here is: use your head, and think ahead. **There is positively no free lunch**, no matter how hard you squeeze your hope. Hope only goes so far.

You have brains in your head.
You have feet in your shoes.
You can steer yourself any direction you choose.

Dr. Seuss

Law of Unintended Consequences

But, I didn't mean for that to happen!—With hands over your eyes, you realize that this is a genuinely a bad situation that will not go away, no matter how hard you pray.

Praying doesn't work after the fact. You may pray for the best outcome considering the circumstances.

Consider: you still have moving boxes laced all the way up your stairs. You are going to finish emptying the boxes and get rid of them next week. Grandma comes by to see your new digs, she trips on a box on the stairs, and falls. **No one wants** to see grandma laying on the floor at the bottom of their stairs. Such a risk had never entered your mind. You're going to be care-sitting for Gram for some time.

This is when two **Laws** gang up on you at the same time: **Law of Gravity**, the **Law of Unintended Consequences**. Talk about complicated!

Remember Gram? Remember, that she is only picked up when the ambulance arrives?

You'll only bring yourself heartache if you try to defy these laws. There are dark forces behind some of the combinations of laws.

"What goes up must come down.
Spinning wheel got to go round."

Lyrics by Earth, Wind, and Fire

Law of Multiplication

Things multiply in the dark.

Just because you can't see it or understand it, that doesn't keep it from happening.

Examples

hangars	plastic containers	cans	mildew
storage boxes		bottles	mice
unmatched socks	pens	insects	tee shirts
electronic cords	cups	mold	ball caps
	souvenirs	magazines	

—and so much more—they multiply—in the dark.

This is a ruthless and unbending law that takes place behind your back. It's worse than zombies taking up residence. (It could have been vampires. At least vampires dress well and are romantic. But no.)

The Law of Inertia or the Procrastinator's Law

Couch potato: A body at rest stays at rest; a body has indisposition to motion, exertion, or change.

A body on the couch can stay on the couch for so long that he/she[1] makes a body imprint, so when this person does get up, he/she will be sucked into the vortex of potatoism, and the he/she becomes a certified *couch potato*.

> **Procrastination:** to put off intentionally the doing of something that should be done, to put off something habitually.

A young body is a terrible thing to waste. A young mind is a terrible thing to waste. There are no re-dos on any hour or day that has passed, and it happens very quickly, without your notice.

A decision made by default is still a decision.

The adage: **The hardest door to open is your own**, continues to prove out. **You** decide if you live a life of consciousness and activity, or a life of unconsciousness and devices. (You know what I mean.) You are the only one who can decide. This decision shouldn't be made by default.

• •

Maritime Law

Time and tide wait for no man. Life's natural cycles don't wait for any human.

• •

Is it your plan to spend your precious life and time tied to the couch, TV, or computer? Is it your plan to make a habit of

---

1 he/she: yes, being politically correct is hard on word flow. We need a new single word for he/she.

being late? Do you often say: just a minute, which could mean up to 12 hours? Do you often say: huh, or when did that happen? Do you let food wrappers pile up around you, rather than expending the effort to take them to the trash?

The hands of the clock move forward whether you do or not. Tick tock. You were younger and better looking yesterday.

* * *

Law of Right to Know

To be made aware of the truth or factuality of; being in accordance with what is just, good, true, or proper.

* * *

Good idea: tell the person to whom you are engaged that you started dating someone else. Tell a guest that the things growing in your refrigerator are not good to eat. Consider money and friends, keep some things private. Loaning money drags one into the **Right to Know**, and **Right to Privacy—give** what you can, be it $20 instead of $2,000. Tell your partying partner that you want to have a baby. Tell a potential sexual partner that you have a disease.

You can always try to break this law. For a little while you think you got away with it. However, (you know this) be warned that it will **always** fly back up like a rock pinched by a tire, and it will smack you hard, between the eyes. It is a merciless, unbending law that waits for the right time to exact a great deal of pain, and leaves a bad mark on your record.

Law of Sexual Reproduction

The process by which plants and animals give rise to offspring; sexually motivated phenomena or behavior.

Everybody Knows This!!!
Why does it even have to be said???

If you **have the vaguest idea you are pregnant**, abstain for a few days until you can take the PG test. It won't hurt you to replace a drink with a soda until you know. You don't have to tell anyone what you're drinking. Ever.

I'm going to step right out here with a radical suggestion. If you want babies, find a partner who wants them too. See if you like each other first. If you are married and ready for babies, joyfully go forth.

If you are not ready for kids, or lackluster relationships, or sexually transmitted disease—*shove the hormones aside and think.* Think about your future, and the future of your child.

It would be hard to find **a law more tested**, and failed. Prayer after intercourse is not birth control. However, if you are pregnant, prayer is appropriate.

Accidental babies are not proof of love or masculinity or femininity. However, they can be welcomed, taken care of, and loved. They do not deserve to be wallowing on the floor in dirty clothes at Local-mart, and yelling for attention, while the parent(s) wander around like zombies and wear pants that defy logic.

Notice

Babies come from unprotected sex. This will change **EVERYTHING** in your life—forever.

Warning

If a woman drinks or does drugs while pregnant, she will unconsciously or purposefully choose to **disable her child.** This is the most serious of bad marks, right in there with fathering a child and **skipping out.**

Many will be downright incensed by these observations, although if one uses **any** logic there is no valid argument. But, I get it. Nobody **means** to. Not meaning to doesn't matter later. *Politically Correct Police*, put out your own handbook, but don't message me.

Law of Attraction/Law of Opposites Attract

Like attracts like: force or action drawing two like things together.

Opposites attract: force or magnetic power draws two opposites together.

What is a person supposed to do? Sorry, you're on your own here. Trusting your gut and heart will not be helpful here.

Law of Luck

A force that brings good fortune or adversity; favoring chance.

Some people appear to be lucky. They always win. They always *get away with it*. We believe strongly that some people are given the gift of *luckiness* and some are *not*.

> "I know he's a good general, but is he lucky?"
>
> N. BONAPARTE

We tend to envy the lucky ones. However, at a most unexpected time, like a pin that pops a balloon, the lucky person will be gobsmacked. (That's a great British expression.) The lucky ones don't have any experience in handling failure. They are derailed. The rest of us have our own hard-won experience and we are more resilient. Depending on luck versus skill is a risky thing to do—and after a time, Bonaparte figured that out.

Next, we will try to find wisdom and humor in the ability to control—well, not much of anything.

> There is no such thing as inner peace. There is only nervousness or death. Any attempt to prove otherwise constitutes unacceptable behavior.
>
> FRAN LEBOWITZ

Control Center On the Street Where You Live

You can't control the outside world,
or even a parking spot.

Control: (to attempt) to exercise power and authority over a business, a relationship, a car, or even a computer.

Surroundings: the circumstances, conditions, or objects by which one is surrounded; your personal environment.

> "In this world there are going to be people that it's better you not be around. Unfortunately, sometimes it is your family."
>
> OVERHEARD SAYING

You can't control the prices of things, you can control what you buy. You can't control politics, you can be knowledgeable. You can't control other people, you can control yourself - maybe.

While it's really unlikely that you will be able to bring order to your job, or your love life, or a grand and worthy cause—you do have some control over your living room.

Your living environment choices of cleanliness levels are:

✓ fanatic   ✓ messy

✓ clean   ✓ hoarder mess

✓ mostly cleanish

I know! More choices. It can be the down side of *freedom*.

In this case, we speak to keeping your home as a place where you are glad to go when the world is roughing you up.

> **Sensibility:** awareness of and responsiveness toward something, in this case where you will live; sensibilities can be emotional, practical, or as yet uncovered; an individual's sensibilities rarely change.

Decide what your eyes like to look at, and what hurts your eyes.

> "I wear my sunglasses at night."
>
> SONG

When it comes to your living space, it's good to know what offends your sensibilities and try to avoid such situations. Be self-aware enough to know if loud noise (or whatever) makes you crazy. No one needs to know you're crazy. We're all crazy in our own way too. (Not kidding.) Determine how much chaos you can handle, and plan accordingly.

If noise bothers you, your first priority should be to find a place that is reasonably quiet. This is probably **not** near a main through-way, or a child-care center, or a bar, or a construction site, or a kennel, or mass transit, or a skate-board park, or a basketball court, or a truck depot. (You may sense noise is on my crazy button/panel.) It's not easy to find a place, but it is absolutely worth the search for those who are sensitive or made anxious by noise.

Acknowledge Your Crazy Button, or Crazy Panel of Buttons

If the **smell** of other people cooking cabbage, sausage, fish, or muktuk bothers your nose, test for hallway smells when you check out a place to rent or buy.

If you need to live near your **family/tribe**, school, or work, your choices are narrowed to a specific area.

If **safety** is a paramount concern for you, you may need to live where you are on an upper floor, and where there is limited access to the building, and low crime in the area.

If you're not into **kids**, you'll want a place more suited to adults. If you are into kids, you'll want a place friendly to them.

If you are afraid of **pets**, or don't like their smell, you'll want a no-pets facility.

If you love to **party**, you won't appreciate having to take care of a yard and flower beds, or neighbors calling the police on your party.

If you love the **city**, try it out. You may not be able to deal with the crowding and noise.

If you love the **country**, try that out. You may not be able to deal with the quiet and lack of action.

If you are **religious**, you may want to live near your church or congregation.

If you're an **artist or designer**, you're probably dying to find an artist's loft in the middle of the action. (Noise-sensitive people, walk away.)

If you're **musical**, you'll want to find a place where you can practice without the police showing up.

If you hate **elevators** and small spaces, plan accordingly.

If you're in **school**, you'll probably have to take what you can get. There are places that encourage studiousness, and places that encourage parties. You choose.

If you think of yourself as **sane**, you probably don't want to live near a crazy person. Crazy is one thing. Certifiably insane is another.

Maybe a **group** of you will look for an apartment where you can all have units. Consider the lay-out, and where you would prefer to be in your unit.

If you need **space**, and want to garden, you probably won't want to live where the cool weather is unfriendly to plants.

If you would not appreciate a **family of 13** living in the two bedroom apartment next door, keep looking. If you **love kids**, you would be an asset to the place.

If you like your place to be **cozy**, you might consider a mobile-home. These mobile-home living areas have a lot of different personalities, so see if you would be a good fit.

If you want to build a **cabin** in the woods, nothing else will do.

If you need an **ocean** beach or a lake—well, good luck.

If you are a **heat** and hot-weather person, you'll, hate it where it's cold.

If you love the **cold**, and sweat when the temperature crawls past 62 degrees, go north.

If you love the **mountains**, you won't be happy in the flat lands.

If you need lots of **light**, you'll need bigger windows. If you prefer your place to be **dark**, you might consider a basement apartment.

She was happy. Too happy...

If you don't know what you are—surprise! This is a good time to think about it.

You are **not going to be perfectly happy** with any place.

Many young people have to take what they can get. This can lend itself to some interesting or creative apartments. That doesn't mean it has to be awful. A good scrubbing, a can of paint, and some fabric, and a few rugs can bring out a livable space in most places. Use your artist's eye.

If you have to live in a dangerous area, try to at least find a place at the outer range of the threat.

Some people only want what they can't have. That's a tough one. So, the want-versus-need people will get high-centered on affordable-versus-not-affordable. If this is you, your friends may stop answering your messages.

Make yourself a list of what works for you and what does not. You may not be able to afford the perfect place, but you could get close. Over this, you do have some control.

See "Personal Credo" on page 139.

Now we'll go to that special place, the joys of roommates.

The Joys of Roommates—or—Don't Let 'Freddie' Move In

(it's not nearly as glamorous as the movie)

Roommate: one of two or more persons sharing the same room or living quarters, also called *roomie,* among other things.

Certain aspects of moving and roommates can be more tricky than you might expect.

Here the **Law of Opposites Attract** shines at its most exhausting brightness. You should know by now that **Murphy's Law** will **always** be present and give you a run for your money. If you are a romantic, or soft-hearted, or BFFFFF, or working for world peace, or have relationship-stars in your eyes, you will not be able to stop yourself. You may not be in a position to choose your roommate! Yikes! Don't panic until its time.

But, first, consider the following.

Chaos vs Order

We have established that your house will neither clean itself, nor will it organize itself. And few roommates will. Decide your tolerance level at both ends of the clean scale, **chaos and germs** or **ultimate order and dominance**. You'll be surprised to find out how many chaos and order people are out there. We all claim to love that gentle line that runs down the middle, but for the most part, people collect at the fanatical ends.

Law of You Can't Change People

If you need order in your life, and you have a roommate who doesn't, there is a well-known but unwritten **Law** that says: **You Can't Change People**. *It's not written down because no one wants to see it.* No one wants to admit they dream of changing their partner, and have listed the ways in a notebook.

The **Law** about changing is probably one of the most difficult rules to take to heart. But, you don't believe it, yet. The odds are probably one in a thousand that you will succeed in bringing about change in someone else. That one chance will be enough to keep most of the Fixers on their quest to fix.

> **Golden saying:** The definition of crazy is doing the same thing over and over and expecting different results.

That's why you simply don't hear the Universe **yelling** in a loud voice: **"You can't change people!"** You can't be changed.

You'll save yourself a lot of pain if you respect this law. But, I respect your need to try, and try, and try and cry, and cry, and cry.

So, when you pick up the roommate's wet towel that has permanently water-damaged your grandmother's antique table, the best you are likely to get back is a shrug, and, "Whatever. It's old."

Facing such lack of respect for you and your belongings is infuriating. You can't make him/her feel bad because they don't feel! Now you realize that you two are not a good roommate match. Screaming and passive aggression will not help, seriously. It will only succeed at entrenching which rarely works out. Maybe one in a thousand odds.

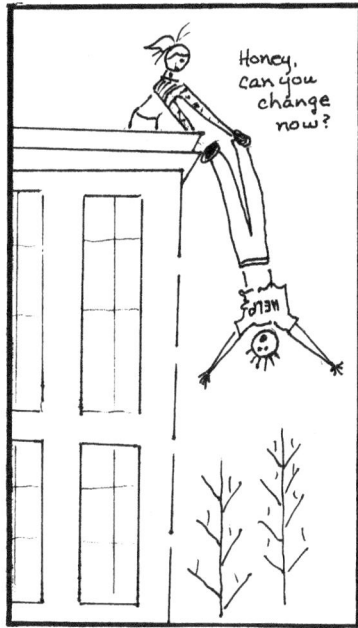

Entrenching: to dig or occupy a trench for defensive purposes.

Think of world wars fought in *trenches*. Each side digs in and prepares to defend their lives. You'll get them out of that trench "over their dead body." That's a fairly strong indication that the only changing that will go on here is change of partners. Does anyone really win? That's how far it can go. Calling the police won't help—unless things get physical.

Seriously, getting physical is a *relationship deal breaker*, period. No second chances. Leave your stuff, go, and be happy to escape with the rest of your life. No joke.

BFF Roommates

The most shocking roommate situation can come from your BFF-FFF. You've been planning and dreaming of moving in together for years. What could be more compatible and wild and fun and free?

However, moving in together changes the dynamics of your relationship. With the advent of limited income, bills, and housing costs, transportation costs, and food costs, you turn into your parents! (I asked you to turn off the lights! You left the gas tank empty! You're running the air conditioner too much! Where is my 1% goat milk?)

Suddenly you will start to wonder vaguely if some of the things your parental units were trying to shove down your throat (about food, money, cars, jobs, laundry, electricity) might have some whiff of validity. That would make some of the other things they told you suspiciously, and possibly, accurate. I'm sorry. I know this is terrible news for you.

There is a reality show that says: I killed my BFF. No kidding. Roommates fall in lust for the same person. I don't know why. They just do. Leave before it gets to that.

You and your BFF roommate(s) move in together, and the conversations start to take a bent and tone you've never heard before. It will become a crime to leave the top off the bottle of shampoo. It will be a higher crime to sing in the morning. You'll debate on which is the right way to install the toilet paper roll, because there has to be some earthly order. More important will be the position of the toilet seat. Yes, that battle rages on. Lid

down, lid up, seat up, seat down —you can see how important this is.

One of you leaves crumbs on the counter, the other uses antibacterial wipes at an alarming rate. The percent of fat in milk, or use of soy milk can become a bitter battle. (Suggestion: buy both kinds.) **Warning! Danger!** Don't eat your roommate's special food unless you're ready for World War III. And wars take an awful lot of energy, and never fully resolve. Is that how you want to live?

Fair Share

The fair share dilemma always follows. One of you will be a spender, and one of you will be a saver. One of you will eat more than the other. One will be into healthy food but sneak the other's junk food, making the junker furious when the cookie box is empty. One of you will never pick-up the mail. One of you will use the others' toothpaste and leave the tube in their bedroom. One of you will lose your job. One of you will ruin the other's sweater. One will never have their share of the rent on time. Someone will eat the last piece of banana bread the other was saving. Some will eat the other's gift chocolates! One of you will want their new and fabulous partner to stay over-night—forever. *See "Roommate Agreement" on page 45.* The other will want one roommate and peace and quiet, and nothing loud on TV. One will love perfume, the other will be allergic.

Soon, you may worry that your BFF has been replaced by an alien. You're analyzing the up-and-down-side of unfriending him or her.

The difference is—you are both using your own money. You are being inconvenienced. (No, not that!) Everything takes on a different flavor when you're paying for it from your wallet—including housekeeping. You can see that there are endless things to argue about. Food, dishes, rent, utilities, boyfriends, girlfriends, towels, pizza, laundry, wine, sodas, yogurt, the bathroom, bills, cleaning, cats, decorations, and so much more.

Morning Person vs Not-Morning Person

However, one of the greatest collisions comes between morning people, and not-morning people. One is cheerful, singing, fixing breakfast. The other is like Dracula. Any light, sound, smell, shortage, or break in their routine can set them off like a fire siren. Together, neither of you is happy, but the cheerful person usually learns to be quiet and stay out of the way because it is so un-fun to start the day with a raging Dracula. After time and coffee, Dracula will probably become human again. Until the next morning.

Here we circle back to the **Law of You Can't Change People**. Dracula will not become sunny, and Happy will move.

My wish for you is that you find the greatest pairing of room-mates ever. Still, it's a good idea to work out a **Roommate Agreement**.

Roommate Agreement

I NEED A CANE

SILLYNESS IS SERIOUS!

it's a look

Potatoes would have worked

Wanna Play?

With memories of our previous roommates experiences, I'm going to suggest that roomies get together and write a **Roommate Agreement**. It is about setting boundaries of what is okay and what is not okay in your living space and life. It doesn't have to be a three inch thick binder like **Big Bang Theory**. (There are many examples, good and bad, on the internet.) You choose the things that are important to you. After reading this, you should have a pretty good idea of what sets you off. Include your deal breakers.

You may as well hash some of this out before the move. It probably won't work, but at least you tried. Not disclosing certain personal quirks (allergic to all fruit, secret lover, preference to sleep on the couch, hugger, hug hater, bad singer, towel dropper) could be considered breaking the **Law of Right to Know**. And you know what a twister that can be.

You will save yourself a lot of life drama, time, and frustration if you push away the desire to try and **Change or Fix the Roomate**.

For instance, I'm sure to have said some things in this book that you don't like. You might even want to yell at me. I accept you just the way you are. Just don't text me.

Couples Moving in Together— Yeah or Nay

Fair warning— Politically Correct, or Incorrect

I can't cover all the kinds of roommate/romance relationships out there, between males and females and so on, without failing to miss someone's combination. So please don't take offence if I settle on the traditional "he and she." If you do take offense, you should probably lobby for some all-inclusive words we can use in their place. Please don't feel the need to let me know. I'll find out and be happy for us all if you succeed.

Casual Move-In

How does the casual move-in start? Over popcorn and beer one Tuesday night, you both think moving in together is an okay idea. I mean, you don't hate each other or anything. This usually comes up after a few days or weeks of romance, followed by a lackluster but mostly comfortable relationship.

Moving early while in a *romantic-like relationship,* will **change everything, long term**. It will seem convenient, maybe even pleasant.

If you're desperate, you may not have much choice. However, if you're shooting for convenience, and someone to share the bills, you're in the right place.

Soon you realize he is proud of his farts. Soon he will realize that you are addicted to romantic novels, and are crabby if your reading is interrupted.

You didn't realize he likes to run around in his boxers and athletic socks. He didn't know you have a thing about how the dishwasher should be loaded.

You graduate to eating too many candy bars, crispy treats, and brownies. This feels pretty okay.

The catch: (Please see every advice column ever written!!!) At some point one will want to be married, and the other won't. One will want to have a child, and the other person says: no, or whatever. That **never** goes well. Two children and three years later, you get married to get the *marriage-fight* off the table.

You are bored. (In a sense, so is everybody.) It's the age where you to want to do what you're not doing. The kids are treasures, but they are a lot of work. It may come down to a showdown over the laundry. So by year four, one of you commits a relation-ship 'deal-breaker.' Then you go into the blame game which usually gets ugly. There is so much mud available to sling. (Monkeys do that.) Suddenly living without the other seems more convenient. You can get the statistics on *Bing.*

It's a confusing world for the kid's afterword. A seven year old boy recently said to me: "I really want a dad. Mine is gone." Then he said: "I have to take really good care of my mom so I won't be an orphan."

His exact words. You decide.

Right to Privacy

Yes, privacy is a precious right and privilege!

Close the Curtains!

Pick up any news about anywhere in the world and you will see terrible examples of others having no right or respect of privacy. By far and away most people in the world **do not**. We in the USA are losing (some would say we **have** lost) the grip on ours. Everything, true or not true—right or incorrect—is in the **Information Cloud**.

Believe it or not, money institutions of the past did not have the ability to know what was is in your heart, let alone your pink piggy bank. Now institutions proudly offer borrowers free FICO scores. How nice. They don't do it for you.

Quiet people, the ones who have nothing to hide, want privacy. Complicated people want privacy. Spies want privacy, right along with other security agencies. Icky people want privacy. How about you?

No one needs to know everything about you. You will have much more fun with your life if they think they know you, but they aren't sure.

Privacy, in this case, comes closer to home and is not so delicate.

Shut the bathroom door!

Knowing everything about each other's bodily habits, cleaning habits, pimples, and other functions can be a real relationship strainer. Think. Don't make me spell it out any further!

Shut the blinds when you're undressing or being sexually active.

No one needs to know your personal—business. And, there are a lot of weirdoes out there. If you like being filmed, videoed, and don't mind icky people watching you—well, okay then. I don't understand, but I am not the Sex Police.

These observations are probably far too conventional for many of you. I'm not the marriage police or the roommate police. I'm simply suggesting that you to **think before** you share your wonderful self with the world.

Don't text me. (A ten year old wants to handle my messages, and he's a little young to handle inflamed language.) Remember, this is an information monologue, not a debate.

No secrets 4 u! #

> "So never be anxious about the next day, for the next day will have its own anxieties. Each day has enough of its own anxieties.
>
> Matthew

Moving Out and In

woot—woot

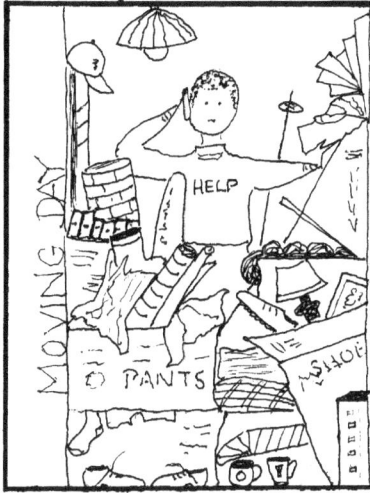

Definition of Moving: one that moves or sets something in motion; the activity of moving of household goods from one residence to another.

Stuff: materials, supplies, equipment, building material, textiles, clothes, shoes, coats, books, jewelry, collections, electronics and their cords, food, drink, clean products, baskets; the contents of whole rooms and buildings.

You probably haven't lived long enough to learn from your mistakes.

Murphy's Law of Moving

If you've helped others move, you have an idea of the drill. If you have chosen not to help others move, you most likely won't find anyone available. They'll be unable to get to their messages. (Don't tell me these phones/pads aren't good for some things.) There is a **rule** out there that says:

You Scratch My Back and I'll Scratch Yours.

Applicable Laws

Law of Multiplication

Law of Diminished Returns

Law of Gravity

Law of Right to Know

Law of Attraction

Law of Unintended Consequences

Rule of Renting

If no one responds to your texts, Lucy, you've got some planning to do. And some money to spend. Some people would actually hire movers. It's a good deal if you can afford it.

As you can see, this is a heavy or weighty subject. Literally and figuratively... You're moving OUT and IN. The natural and unnatural laws and rules go into hyper-drive here.

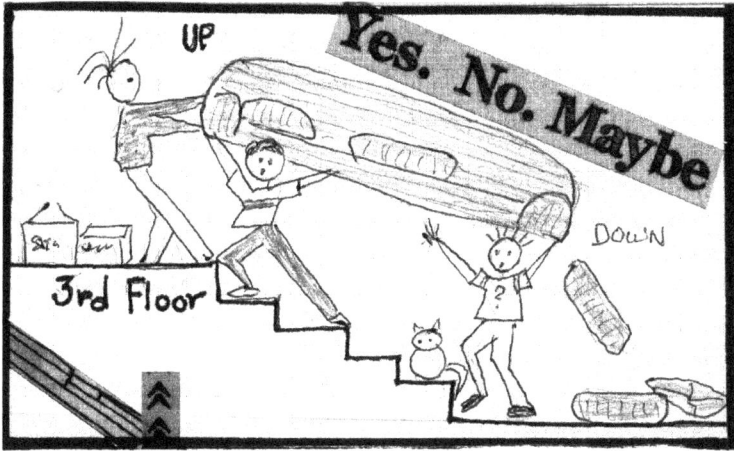

Home: residence, family unit, domestic space, domicile, house, apartment, condo, mobile home, room, box, base camp.

Help: to give assistance or support to; one that helps, especially with manual labor; in this case, commonly family or friends.

Some of you have broad experience in taking care of a home, and some of you none. Learning, and more important, **accepting** that nothing will be perfect, or exactly what you expect, will go a long way toward managing your home, your expectations, and your sanity.

Now, some people are happy as can be in the middle of a mess. God bless them, because you can't and shouldn't try to fix it for them. They are happy. It's their life.

It is helpful to know that there are people out there who love nothing more than to attack the mess and forcibly bring order to chaos. And if you want that kind of help, those people are better than gold. The problem is, they are hard to find.

Hopefully, you are blessed by having such a person in your life. However, they will be annoying. Anyone who is good at organizing and cleaning will always be annoying. It's the **Rule of Organizers**. By now you might be thinking, if the author calls something a rule, she might have a reason.

"I saw that I had been living with a self-centered sense of unimportance…"

NANCY COLLINS

New Place Logistics and Landlords

The Landlord is always scary.

You've found a place that will be your nest, your home base, your base camp, for some time to come. You've got a group of people committed to help you move, paid or unpaid. Most likely you are renting, unless you've got parental units with big bucks to buy you a condo. Not likely, but possible.

It would be helpful for you to have a *little, tiny sketch* of a **plan for your move**. Yeah, logistics!

> **Logistics:** procurement, maintenance, facilities, personnel and transportation (often military) for a specific project.

Maybe you could make some lists! I know, it's a commitment, but maybe you could spend a couple of bucks on a new notebook with a flap and keep all your *moving* paperwork and lists in there. Perhaps you could use 'notes' on your i-phone-pad-camera-tablet-berry. I know. I ask too much. But what about this *stuff?*

??What-About This Stuff??

- ✓ times
- ✓ *moving dates*
- ✓ deposits
- ✓ utilities
- ✓ payments
- ✓ square-footage
- ✓ *keys*
- ✓ furnishings
- ✓ pantry
- ✓ *nearest emergency room*
- ✓ landlord rules
- ✓ boxes labeled with contents

- ✓ contacts
- ✓ small appliances
- ✓ where you want your furniture
- ✓ contracts
- ✓ addresses
- ✓ phone numbers
- ✓ confirmations
- ✓ phone/internet
- ✓ movers
- ✓ *food and drinks for movers*
- ✓ *weather*
- ✓ entrance to building

- ✓ where you'll park while moving in
- ✓ bed/couch/ entertainment-center size
- ✓ *door size and stair width!*
- ✓ walk-through
- ✓ notifications
- ✓ anxiety meds
- ✓ willing friends
- ✓ hired movers
- ✓ self mover
- ✓ deadline getting out
- ✓ deadline moving in

If these topics have never run through your mind, you're not a planner. Maybe you could try planning, or better yet, find that friend we talked about—the one who is a planner or logistician, and ask them to help, just this once.

Feeding the Movers—No Exception!!!

Friends Help Friends is a Rule: or, if you feed them they will come. If you feed them more, they will stay. I cannot believe that some people do not know this! Drudgery is mitigated by food. No food, no workers.

Remember, your people are giving up their precious hours to help you. **They don't have to.** No one is standing out there saying: I can't wait to help Johanna or Terrinance to move, or—I'm looking forward to building Alexandrey's deck, or—I really want to help dig out LaRonald's dead trees, or—I can't wait to help carry Aldonna's leather couch and entertainment center up three flights of stairs.

Praise your wonderful helpers, no matter how weird their names are. Tell them they are beautiful, and move on. And, don't ever take them for granted.

I've actually been there when the person being moved failed to provide food and drink. It's embarrassing. The movers whisper to each other: where's the food? The person being moved does not have water, let alone a clue. The one being moved might even say, "Will someone order pizza?" and then, let the person who ordered pay! (Don't fall for this!)

Shortly, one by one, the mover-helpers will leave for important unexpected appointments. And the cheese stands alone.

Unwritten Rule

You get to **eat anything you want on moving day**. That is why it is doubly disappointing if there is nothing bad to eat. And those cheap yellow cookies from the sale rack don't hack it.

Donuts, pizza, taco packs, chips, burgers, dogs, cookies, water, sodas, beer, coffee, iced tea, and brownies will be consumed in mass quantities.—**Just plan and budget for it**, or you'll never be able to move again without a moving company. Price that.

Exit Plan

FIRST MOVE

WISH U WERE HERE

Now, you're REALLY moving OUT, and you, who are already renting, didn't pay any attention to the *text of your rental agreement*. Yikes! The place has to look like it did when you moved in or you don't get your rental deposit back. (The rental deposit can be a lot of money.)

One thing at a time. If you're leaving your folks place they will probably be so glad to see you go that you can leave dust bunnies, computer cords, posters, and old underwear, and they'll just say: "Bye!"

If you are not leaving your parental unit's home, you'll pretty-much have to clean up the place for the exit with the landlord.

You might have let this cleaning thing become a monster to you. But when your place is empties out, the things that need to be done are clearer, and you don't have to move anything to do it. That's half the battle.

Turn on the music or sports or an action movie, and go for it. For being so low on your to do list, you will feel relief and satisfaction when your place is clean. (You even changed that light bulb that hasn't be working for a year).

Carpentry skills and the drive to fix-it become highly valued by others. Maybe you'll find you're good at this. Not that many people are. There is almost a reverence for the person who confidently steps in and knows how to do everything, and fixes all those broken things. These people are to be treasured and treated with respect.

As you prepare to do the 'big clean,' you should own, or have rented, or have borrowed much of this:

✓ Vacuum and extra bags

✓ Carpet cleaning machine

✓ Broom(s)

✓ Scrub brushes, various sizes

✓ Bucket

✓ Paper towels

✓ Rags/wash cloths

✓ Newspaper (set grubby stuff on it)

✓ XL Plastic Bags

✓ Dust pan

✓ Screw drivers: Phillips, and straight

✓ Case knife and spackle

✓ Hammer

✓ Nails and tacks

✓ Wall cleaning sponges

✓ Toilet and tub cleaner

✓ Oven cleaner

✓ Dish detergent

✓ Microfiber mop

✓ Vinegar (ALL purpose anti-germ cleaner)

What!? Are you kidding! That's a lot of stuff!

Now is **not the time** to have an asthma attack, a nervous breakdown, a migraine, or cramps.

Okay, short list:

- ✓ Dish detergent & vinegar if you know how to use it
- ✓ Broom with soft brush
- ✓ Wall cleaning sponges, and old towels
- ✓ Wipes: plain, anti-bacterial, counter top and glass
- ✓ Vacuum/carpet cleaner
- ✓ Plastic bags
- ✓ Toothpaste and brush
- ✓ Oven cleaner

Bring your breathing back to normal. You can do this bite by bite. Don't try and eat the whole sandwich at once. First, get the place cleared of everything but cleaning tools.

Tackle main chores separately. If you're the type that has to keep going, plan for a full day. If you like to break chores up, estimate how long it will take you to do each chore and plan accordingly. It works well to tackle surfaces in groups that need the same tools. Jell-O, welded to the inside of the refrigerator by time, is going to take some time to soak and scrape off. This list depends on how bad you've let things get:

- ✓ Floors of all kinds
- ✓ Walls and ceiling
- ✓ Doors inside and out
- ✓ Kitchen counters and cabinets
- ✓ Refrigerator
- ✓ Bathroom fixtures
- ✓ Windows
- ✓ Deck and/or porch
- ✓ Steps

If you have out-door space, such as a deck, or porch, or a yard, that space is its own category.—Hey, you're the one who wanted a deck and a lawn. They are outside rooms that need as much work as any indoor rooms.

A clean, *soft* broom is a good, fast scrub-brush for the shower and tub, especially if you forgot to get that long-handle brush I recommended. It works better if you wash the broom before and after using it on each chore! It's not good to drag mud and germs from one place to the next.

After sweeping or vacuuming hard floors, the soft broom can also be used to scrub the tile or vinyl. Get your broom wet with hot soapy water and go after that floor. Wipe up the soap and water on the floor using the 'foot' method—put towels on the floor and pretend you're skiing. This is pretty fast. Or—

A microfiber mop makes fast work of windows, walls, and floors too. Buy a couple extra fiber pads and just keep it clean!

Use the vacuum hose around all the edges of the floors, vents, and hard to reach areas. Find a narrow hose nozzle that will reach under the appliances.

Dish detergent can cover most of your soap needs, but vinegar is best for windows and is a good germ fighter. See, isn't that great?

If the vinyl floor took a couple dents, you can carefully fill them in with a couple coats of similar color nail polish—really.

I know. *This 'scrubbing' bit is terrible news.* **It is clearly better to keep that rental agreement in mind when you move in.** Still, you have choices: clean as you go, allow time to deep clean, hire cleaning people, or lose your deposit.

Seriously, if you're too busy, if you cannot bring yourself to lift a broom, or toilet brush—give up Americanos, lattes, baseball cards, latest multi-upgrades, vinyl finger and toenails, and *hire someone* to clean for you. It's worth it doing without your favorites for a little while.

Landlord Inspection

Oh, oh...

Eyeball offenders[1] to look for before the landlord arrives for final inspection. Picture this:

- ✓ you were practicing with your numb-chucks and gouged the wall

- ✓ your man-cave demanded that you try and hang an airplane prop on your wall, and you couldn't find the stud so the wall is all chewed up

- ✓ you forgot to open the chimney flue, and made a romantic fire, and smoked the place up

- ✓ you were dancing in your high heels, and dug a hole in the flooring

- ✓ you burnt something vile and immovable in the bottom of your oven, or under the stove-top burners

- ✓ you dumped a bag of sugar or flour in the cupboard and never got around to cleaning it up

- ✓ you made a practice jump into your bean bag and it exploded and there are magnetic foam dots everywhere

---

1   When you sign your new rental agreement, it's a good idea to do a checklist for damage or wear in your new place before moving in. You do this so you don't get dinged for damage you didn't do upon moving out.

✓ someone was standing on your table trying to change a light bulb, and put their head through the ceiling

✓ the air conditioner accidentally fell out of the window

✓ you hung ten or twelve posters or pieces of art (or chains, or cables, or signs, or light strings, or duct tape) on your walls and the pattern shows like an array from Star Wars

✓ you built yourself a canopy bed using gauze and tacks in the ceiling

✓ your screen door won't shut and it used to

✓ light fixtures or light bulbs are broken

✓ there was a leak under your sink, and you never got around to telling the landlord about it, and now the floor is soft and squishy

✓ you still have boxes and bikes and brooms and dead plants on your front steps

✓ your towel bar has been hanging sideways since two weeks after you moved in, and most of the light bulbs are burnt out

✓ you won't walk in your own home barefoot

✓ you close your eyes when you go to the toilet

There is nothing new under the sun.

You say: This is not funny. Make it stop.

Tackle with Spackle

The more sophisticated way to repair holes in the wall is to buy mixed spackle at any place that sells paint or building supplies (and probably the grocery market). It comes in yogurt size containers and is very inexpensive. You might need wall-repair-mesh if you took out a chunk of sheetrock. *Read the directions*, and fill the small holes on your walls using a putty knife or a case knife. Read the directions and put the mesh over the bigger hole(s) and use the putty and knife. It's just not that hard.

Note

Toothpaste must be white, and it does not work to cover places where you put your ski pole or your head through the wall.

Emergency Spackle

In case of emergency, (the landlord will be here in a half hour), you suddenly see nail holes everywhere—there is a short-cut. You may fill those little tack/nail holes with white (not blue or green or red) *toothpaste*. Put a little on the tip of your finger and fill the holes. Wipe the wall with a damp cloth after the hole is filled.

Before Landlord

Before the x-landlord arrives, step back and look at the empty place you're leaving. Sniff the air—it should not smell of anything but lemon, vinegar, and bleach.

Most landlords don't have a sense of humor about broken things, gouges, a new family of vermin, or mold and mildew. Anywhere.

Not the Whole 9 Yards

It's not possible to give you the whole nine yards of cleaning. If you have a friend who is a clean-freak, beg, yes beg that person to help you. It is likely that you'll ruin something. Did you think this would go perfectly? Read the instructions. Use your head. You have the internet and others to confuse you.

Wet Wipes, You Can Clean the World

Commonly called baby wipes,
but they come in 30 flavors

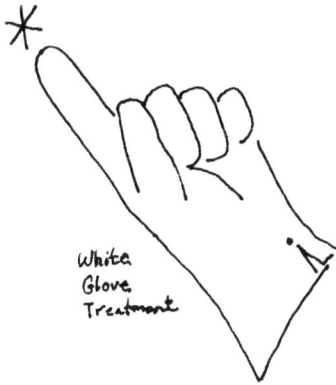

White
Glove
Treatment

Wipe: to rub with something soft for cleaning, to remove by rubbing, to clean by wiping

Cleaning: preparation for cleaning or cleansing; to rid of impurities by washing; free from dirt or pollution; clean from moral corruption

Cleanliness is next to Godliness

There used to be a commercial that said: if you think water is moisture, you're all wet. It was a heavy handed commercial, but it made a certain point. Wet Wipes are the moisture cloths of quick cleaning. But they're not all wet. Just mostly wet. They are your best friend when sticky things go wrong. There was a time before wipes! It was a disaster.

Folk in the action in the military totally appreciate wipes. They are precious. Think about it—hot wind, dust, heat, sand, a ton of gear, sweat, bugs, long days and nights, and no water. Who's your good friend: the one who will share wipes.

With an arsenal of wipes, you can be prepared to meet the various attacks of **Murphy's Law** and lessen the damages. Think of them as great friends, at least part of the time.

I know, you are thinking: wipes, please? I'm not in the military. My friends are people, not wipes.

Consider—you are out and about, and you dump a cup of coffee or a soda or ice cream or energy drink all the way down the front your favorite shirt. A really cute person of the other sex is watching. Your friend is standing beside you laughing. If you have a pack of wipes in your bag, who's your best friend now?

Wipes are damp fibrous sheets of mystery material, about the size of an unfolded tissue—and, there are times when you'd knock your mom out of the way to get to a container of wipes.

Consider: You are at the gas station to fill-up. You just bought an energy drink, and you're on the way to a meeting that is important to you. The last person who used the nozzle for gas left it full, and when you pulled it out, gas went down your legs and the side of your car. Paper towels are not going to hack it here. Now, who's your friend?

You are on the curb waiting for the *walk-light*, you have on your best jacket, and the bus goes by and douses you with muddy water.

You tip the spaghetti sauce you just made, and that stuff seems to have been able to take itself five feet in every direction—it has gone out like an array covering your kitchen counters, cabinets, stove, your hair, your shirt, and the floor. (They rarely make it to the sink. That's too easy.) You were not going for the red-spatter look. Now, you will come to know that spaghetti sauce, left to dry, has the sticking power of atomic glue.

Repeat—Murphy's Law is Versatile

It applies to spilling, dumping, dropping, staining, and smearing, and Murphy is as fit and opportunistic as ever.

Smart you, you grab your handy container of wipes, because the texture and dampness work well in these spill situations. Wipes also work well on sticky, dusty, scary stuff. You will be desperate about a cleaning up a spill around your electronics. This is a time when you would knock your grandmother down to get to the wipes.

And, they work well on children and adults' bottoms! Now, that's a pretty versatile product! They even have wipes for dogs and cats!

You will learn the wisdom (or not) of keeping wipes inside the kitchen and bath, in the car, at your place of work, in your bag. After being out in public, hands touching who knows what, a single pack of sanitary wipes will do a pretty good job of cleaning your hands.

Before you pick up that big fat sandwich between your grubby fingers, wipes seem like a good idea. What? Does your table look like Attila the Hun just ate a gross of bean burritos there? Well, you have a wipe to take care of that so you can safely put your elbows on the table.

(If you don't know who Attila the Hun is, look it up on your search engine. You'll be impressed.) (Alexander the Great is also gruesomely fascinating.)

Because we're perverse, it's kind of fun when these things happen to other people. You have wipes. Now who's smart and popular.

You're in your car, sitting at a light, you decide to take a hurking bite out of your bacon cheeseburger. The light changes, and the middle of burger slides out of the bun hitting your shirt, the shift knob, the seat, and then the floor. (You know the feeling.) You have a box of wipes which tempers your panic.

You're just going to put that soda on the dash for a second. Some idiot pulls in front of you and you hit the brakes. The soda flips three times like a snowboarder. As you swerve down the road, you would trade your great grandmother for some wipes. Pull over. Remember? You have wipes. Now, you'll need window-cleaning wipes.

Who wants a gummy steering wheel, console, seats, and shift knob? Who isn't going to be glad that they kept a pack of wet wipes in their car when their fingers start sticking to the steering wheel?

Environmental Concerns and Wet Wipes

I don't think the "world police" have fully weighed in on which is easier/harder on the environment—wipes, or laundry loads, or wash cloths, or napkins, or mops, or sponges. Most of these cleaning items need to be thoroughly washed and dried, or they turn into repulsive, muddy germ factories. A wipe is another paper product in the trash and out of sight. You decide. Either way you'll feel guilty.

I wrote an article about the wonders of *wipes* for a magazine. One reader, a member of the 'world police,' wrote back to the magazine fairly frothing. According to her, wipes were an environmental hazard and a danger to kids. I would say, it is a hazard to the rest of the world when your germy child, who carries the most virulent strain of cold and flu, gives it to me.

Okay, I'm a little militant about this issue with wipes and flu and colds. We people can be seriously, miserably sick for two weeks out of our very own private lives. It's memorable, and not in a good way. It's not how I want to spend my time.

I was behind a woman with three kids in a grocery cart, and she was picking up a prescription. The snot, and barky coughs, tongues, and sticky hands didn't leave any surface of the cart untouched. (I genuinely felt bad for this mother who was near the breaking point.) But what she left on that cart was a hazard. **World Police of Contagious Illness**, where are you?

Fortunately, most grocery stores now have disinfectant wipes available near the carts so one can clean off the handle bar of the cart or basket. Grab one and save yourself a couple weeks of misery.

The *all-purpose wipes, and baby wipes* are the most widely useful, and least expensive of the group. You can buy them by the case at the box stores. (Yes, really.) Different wipes are available for every kind of cleaning—even the end of the world. *These are a few of what will be your favorite things when the time comes:*

✓ hand-cleaning wipes

✓ eye-glasses wipes

✓ window wipes

✓ antibacterial hand wipes

✓ antibacterial cleaning wipes

✓ floor wipes

✓ kitchen wipes

✓ shop wipes

✓ polishing wipes

✓ vinyl/leather wipes

✓ insect repellant wipes

✓ furniture polishing wipes

✓ dusting wipes

✓ dog and cat wipes

I'm sure I've missed some very important wipes here, and for that I apologize. But I don't want to hear about it.

If you are totally adverse to dirty wash rags/cloths, and dirty buckets of water, then, wipes are probably for you. Baby wipes work well for dusting and cleaning dark corners, and under toasters, and the backs of drawers. And if you don't have children, you get extra environmental-wipe-privileges because you probably don't use mass boxes of disposable diapers for several years.

You may prefer some of the stronger wipes for the floor, the toilet, the counter after raw meat, the grill—I think you've got the idea.

Don't wear a protein drink all day because you didn't have wipes handy.

Kitchen—Tidy or Ptomaine

It can be irritating when your feet stick...

Kitchen: a place or a room with cooking facility; a place where food is prepared

Salmonellosis: food poisoning caused by infection with salmonella organism which are rod-shaped bacterium; usually characterized by gastrointestinal upset, diarrhea, fever, and occasionally death; usually contracted eating undercooked or contaminated food

E. coli: an enterobacterium used in public health as an indicator of fecal pollution

OK!

Does your 'cooking facility' look like a landfill? Are you unable to find/use your sink or stove? Is your refrigerator a stinky, seriously smelly, gooey hazard? Do you have more than one full trash bag of garbage waiting to go out to the dumpster? Do you let your dishes soak for days? Do you spend too much time with the toilet? These are connected.

Dishes and germs are indifferent to human's distress.

It is no longer okay to put dirty dishes under your bed. I'm sorry, neither you nor I have a 'dish fairy' who sweeps through at night. And, eating from dirty dishes can ruin your day/week.

If you simply will not do dishes, you can try the disposable paper plate, plastic cup, and disposable pan route. It's not environmentally sensitive, but it is also not environmentally sensitive to have a health hazard of a kitchen. Can you handle the enviro-guilt? (You still have to take the trash out.)

If you needed to sign some papers, would you have to clear a place on the kitchen floor where you would kneel and sign the papers?

That is scary.

The subject of the kitchen and cooking has filled encyclopedias and books and web sites. We'll cover some of the high points here. If you want recipes or further instructions, you know where to search. We're just hitting the high points. Not that food isn't great.

Applicable Law

Law of Disease and Germs

Law of Multiplication

Murphy's Law

Alert!

It is said that repetition does raise awareness. So, I repeat, handle raw chicken and meat as if you are going in to do surgery. Clean before and after. Salmonella! Botulism! E. coli! Food-born illnesses are nothing to mess with.

More bad news

This applies to all meats and eggs.

Look it up! Or don't.

Check out the *caveat* (remember this word?) at the bottom of many restaurant menus:

"Consuming raw or undercooked meats, poultry, shellfish, or eggs may increase your risk of food-born illnesses."

In English this means: *raw stuff might make you very sick.* Go ahead and try it if you want. It's your stomach and intestines. They won't care if you're in the ER holding a pan and sitting on the toilet.

"While most shoppers assume the uncooked plastic-wrapped bird, sold in the store, is sterile and safe, nothing could be further from the truth. In terms of food safety, it's best to assume that all poultry is **swimming in bacteria** and should be handled accordingly."

RICHARD MARINI

If you'd rather not have food poisoning, you need to be aware of the drips of fluid, starting at the store where you buy meat, fish, and poultry, and all the way home. Double bag your purchase. Keep anti-bacterial wipes handy for drips and sticky fingers.

It's a good idea to get refrigerator stuff in the fridge as soon as possible. Wash up, with hot soapy water, whatever your purchase leaks or drips on from the store to the stove. You will like having a basin of hot soapy water in the sink while cooking, so you can wash often.

Worthy of Repeat

The juices of **raw** chicken, beef, pork, game meat, goat (goat: the most common meat eaten on the planet, for Pete's sake!) and some fish, can make you so sick that you'll think death doesn't look so scary. (How do I know?)

People have safely cooked meat since before you were born! Really. On your device, look up: *cooking, or meat cooking, or how do I know when it is done? Or how do I know if it's not done? Where does an egg come from and how does it work?* (This is a question brought to you by a recent *Survivor* episode.) *Or how do I know if it is spoiled? What does it mean if it smells funny? Is slick meat okay? How long do I need to cook meat to make sure it is safe?* (You can see why I get such good search results.)

The internet and the Bible can take you all the way back to the original barbeque, so I don't have to.

A note for Sushi Lovers: Sushi lovers are generally at very low risk with good preparers who are professionals at food handling. I love it. But, I wouldn't buy it at the stop-and-go store.

You may feel more comfortable wearing disposable gloves when you handle raw meat.

I don't mean to send you all into veganism, but consider stock yards, meat packing plants, fishing boats, massive chicken lots, and muddy barns full of manure. Do you think everything that comes through there can be perfectly processed? Well, it's time to be disillusioned.

Remember the hot soapy water?

Once it's in the pot or on the grill and cooked to the appropriate temperature, it is no longer a land-mine of germs. (Still, clean the meat fork at the first turning.) Life is busy. There are a lot of foods that will turn on you if you leave them sitting out of the fridge for too long, or don't clean them well.

Many fruits and veggies can be tricky too. (I know. This is seriously awful. What can you trust?) Sprouts (yikes), raw milk, raw eggs and egg shells, tomatoes, and melons deserve your attention. It's called food poisoning for a reason. (Look it up.) (Wash it.) (Be paranoid.)

Your clean-up rule should be applied to seafood as well.

Remember this: no food is innocent.

Picture mashed potatoes, spaghetti, cake batter, white sauce, egg, tuna, condiments, and a whole spectrum of drinkables. Picture those sticky things on/in your stove, counters, backsplash, toaster, microwave, and kitchen window and sill. You'll even occasionally hit the ceiling with your topless hot-shot blender or juicer.

Murphy's Law is drawn to the kitchen. So many things can go wrong. Food, knives, contamination, dropsy - uncontrollable food, sauces, drinks, batters, dips—slippery food, dirty hands, and appliances that don't work—see, scary. And yet, kitchens and cooking remain highly in favor.

- Instant Cement -

Making Your Own Cement

The Great Wall of China was cemented with a paste of flour and water. Not really. But it could have been cemented with cooked potato, or uncooked egg, or oatmeal. The sticking and hardening power of these items is legendary. You can immediately survey and clean up a splash with hot, soapy water, or a wipe, in seconds. Or, you can chisel it off later.

Kitchen: Washcloths, Sponges, Scrubbers

If you can't commit to frequent machine-washing in hot water (with a little bleach) of dish cloths, sponges, pot holders, and dish towels, you'll probably have to go 'disposable'. It's your call. Again, you will feel guilty either way. (Who knew these things would be the root of guilt.)

If you cannot commit to washing dishes, cups, utensils, glasses, bowls, and pans, you will want to seek out the disposable units. It's a lot more trash in the landfill, so you have to decide if you can live with that.

If you use sponges and dish scrubbers—*wait, don't*. It is almost impossible to keep them clean.

I was recently frightened by an article reporting that one's dishwasher could be contaminated and needs to be cleaned regularly. I know! No place is safe!

Sanity versus Insanity

With dishes, consider the popular adage: just-do-it. Place all dirty dishes in the dishwasher, or wash them every night before bed. Wipe the counters. Then, in the morning, you get up and there is nothing to go crazy over—well, at least not in the kitchen. This habit could change your life. But it is more likely you'll have to play out a few hundred bouts of *dishes in cold, greasy water, the accompanying fury, and blame—then those same dishes will be waiting when you get back home*—seemingly colder and greasier than before.

Pots and Pans

You will probably use two of the set of eight pots and pans that come in the set. Consider, they are large, hard to store, and get in your way. However, sometimes the set is cheaper than the individual pans. If you inherit these cooking tools, so much the better. You can upgrade later if that is important to you.

If you're watching your budget, and you have the inclination, you can hit the garage sales and thrift stores. Its kind-of addicting when you get really good buys on designer and popular-brand stuff.

If you're committed to a match set, and you can afford it, go for it.

There are people who want their kitchen to look like a professional store display, or a magazine photo. Really. However, that will not be of great importance to the many of you who are living on Raman or mac and cheese.

If You Eat, You May Want Dishes

Many of you will be encouraged to inherit the old dishes from home. If you hate them, don't take them. With your decline, you may want to say you had "something else in mind—but thank you"—rather than saying "those dishes are ugly, and I hate them, gag." It's a matter of style.

There are so many reasonably priced dish sets out there at box stores, and new sets can be surprisingly easy on your budget.

Some people like to match dishes from different sets. If you are into it, you can go with *English cottage and country or Midcentury amoeba, circles, and stars.* Or garage-sale chaos.

When purchasing and recycling dishes, run your hand around the edge of each piece of dishware and check for chips, cracks, and scratches before you buy. If you don't mind chips, disregard.

If you don't have an eye or the desire to mix or match kitchen stuff, (hard to imagine) if you never set down the plate you're eating from, take the ugly dishes and say: "thank you." Later, if you become domestically inclined, hundreds of choices are out there.

Cute Appliances

Keep in mind that small appliances are plentiful at specialty stores, box stores, thrift stores and flea markets. You probably have family and friends with many of these donut maker, pasta

Ridiculously Tempting Appliances

Coffee maker

Hot water/tea kettle

Microwave

Hot plate

Electric fry-pan

Electric grill

Toaster

Toaster Oven (not the same)

Mixer Set with bowls and blades

Blender

Juicer

Timer

Bread-maker

Pots and pans

Eating implements

Cooking implements

Serving implements

Nesting bowls for cooking and serving

Measuring cups and spoons

Set of dishes from dinner plates to bowls

Drinking glasses, wine glasses

Drinking cups and mugs

Beverage serving pitcher

Flatware/silverware

Knives and cutlery

Kitchen wash cloths and hand towels

Placemats and linens

Food storage baskets

Food storage containers and organizers

Cutting boards (plastic vs wood)

Crock pot

Serving platters

Grill

maker, juicer, sandwich press, blender, bread maker, coffee pots, and electric swizzle sticks, tucked in their clothes closet.

"Mom, why do you have a bread maker in your clothes closet?" With that comment, it will probably be yours.

There are deals at thrift stores and garage sales. If you pay $2, you won't be out too much if it doesn't work. There are usually plug-ins so you can see if the lights go on. Take it home and get out the wipes, hot water and soap—it's like new. Then put it in your clothes closet.

1st Rule

If you can't wash it, don't bring it home.

2nd Rule

Nearly everything is washable. But not everything.

Let your hunter-gatherer instincts propel you on this adventure. Remember the ubiquitous bumper sticker that says: I brake for garage sales. These people are serious. If you think you want it, pick it up, and decide as you cruise through the tires and tables. If you're hands aren't on it, it's not yours. Warning, you will be distracted by things you never knew you needed. Guard against becoming a hoarder, if you can.

Do you like to cook, eat out, or do take-out? Make an assessment of what you think you'll need and use in your kitchen. You can add as you go.

Appliances take up a lot of space, but some of them are ridiculously tempting.

Calm your adrenaline down

You really don't need many of these except a microwave, toaster, and kettle. Fill-out your cupboards appropriate to your needs. If you live on take-out you can go for the uncluttered or Spartan look. If you like to cook for others, obviously you'll have more needs. And more needs. And more needs. Then, you might need an intervention.

The story of the toilet and the dish cloth

Yuck! The dirtiest most germy things in a house is said **not** to be the toilet, (although it should be cleaned often)—but kitchen wash cloths and sponges! Change them often, clean them often. Lift the sponge or wash cloth to your nose. If you smell a swamp, it's because it has become a mini-swamp. Most people don't want their dishes or counters to be swamped with germs.

Sidetrack #1—TV remotes, phones, keyboards

TV remotes and phones and keyboards and tablets are grubby little tools too! Think about it. Do you, (or does anyone else), ever wash their hands before using these devices … ever? Do the devices go from the kitchen to the bathroom to the bedroom to the table to the couch to the car to the bus to the diner? … to a child's mouth, the sidewalk, or your coffee cup…

Where were they before they came into your hands? It's okay if you are now a little paranoid. Just hit these devices with an antibacterial wipe with some regularity. You can even claim it as a chore done.

Sidetrack #2—Wipes

There is a whole group of people out there who are ready to rumble over which **type of wipes** must be used when and where…

Yes, really. It's a strange, strange, strange world. *See "Wet Wipes" on page 67.*

Sidetrack #3—Critic Epidemic

We're living through a **"critic epidemic".** There are an incredible number of authorities out there. They all have computing systems. Their best fun is hanging someone out to dry publically, if not usefully. Some people seek controversy and exceptions like others hunt dark chocolate. The opportunity to be corrected by others should never be underestimated. Try not to let it scare you.

Really, how bad can it go? Sometimes you make things work, sometimes you can't. You gotta roll with it and—this is a big one—**manage your expectations**. If you expect to design the perfect kitchen, well, you can't. There is no such thing.

I love saying: Look it up.

Cozy Nest or Dump in the Bedroom

Bedroom: a room furnished with a bed and intended primarily for sleeping.

Closet: a cabinet or recess for clothing and assorted items.

Mirror: something that gives a *true representation*.

● ●

Laws and Rules in the Bedroom

Law requires you to provide clean sheets and towels for any guest staying overnight at your place. The fine is $200 for breaking that law. (It should be.) Wouldn't you want that?

● ●

Law does not require you to keep those pesky tags on your pillows, sheets, mattress pad, or mattress. (Those "don't remove" tags are for the seller, not the buyer.)

It is against the law to sleep on an uncovered mattress. The fine is $500, and there are people out there who get finder fees for turning you in. (*Well, there should be a law.*) There is something about an uncovered mattress that looks trashy. Because it is. Don't message me about this.

You're worried, I can hear you saying: *I know you are ruining my bedroom like you have the other rooms. Now I'll worry about dust and germs in the bedroom and on the bed.*

I am forced to add: and bugs.

The basic bedroom holds a bed and possibly a headboard, bedside table and lamp, a chest of drawers or baskets, a chair, and a closet, a clock, and full length mirror, (no kidding—everyone needs one—no exception).

Minimalists will be happy with a cot, a quilt, a flashlight, a box, and a national flag for window covering.

At the other end of the scale, **maximalists** will want the room coordinated including paint, new bed covers, many pillows, matching trash basket, mirrored side table, matching arm chair, a theme lamp, a floor lamp to go with the chair, a TV, a desk, and rug on top of the rugs. The windows will have their own layered theme. There may even be a little faux-fireplace. There is no doubt there will be a closet organizer of some kind, and a full length mirror in this room.

Then there is the **basic** bedroom, bed from home, chest of drawers from home, side table (TV table, cardboard box),a treadmill with good intentions, a lamp, and a lot of shoes and clothes.

There is a rare subset of bedrooms like that will be kept up. Like I said, rare.

There is something very sad about unmade designer beds, and piles of pillows on the floor. If you're not going to make your bed, all you really need is: a mattress pad, 2 bottom sheets, 2 comforters, 2 pillows, and two pillowcases. Alternate them on laundry day once a week.

This is simplicity.

Simplicity and Serenity

Now, we'll speak to the grand idea of simplicity and serenity. **However, simple isn't simple**, it is carefully managed.

S & S Bedroom Routine: bed made, clothes hung up, shoes on a rack, bags on hooks, undergarments in the chest of drawers or baskets. Readers may need a book case. Dirty clothes are in the clothes hamper. The window blinds should not be see-through, and should close out the light for best sleep. No clutter. No exercise bike or treadmill or ironing board or TV, which is also said to be best for sleep/rest. Look it up!

It is possible.

Bed & Refuge

The bed is the arguably the point of the whole room. You spend a third of your life on your bed. Theoretically. Pre-owned mattresses, unless from someone well known, should be passed over. (Bed Bugs! They're real, gag.)

Air beds are available in all sizes, and usually fit the budget until you're ready to spring for one of the new super-mattresses. (You might start a little savings account with that in mind.) (I know, that's ridiculous.)

Tip on air beds: After you inflate the bed and test it for firmness, do put on a significant mattress pad. A clean sleeping bag can do the job as a pad under the fitted sheet. If you buy a mattress pad, make sure it is a thick one. This is recommended because single sheets against the plastic are cold, and cannot breathe, and so they feel damp. You won't like it. You may even want a foam pad.

As you think about your bed coverings, consider:

✓ Bed—choose the size of the bed you need

✓ Mattress pad

✓ Sheets sets (top and bottom sheet and pillowcase), cotton, fleece, flannel, or knit

✓ Bed covering, comforter, quilt, bedspread, fuzzy blanket

✓ Sleeping pillows (change out every year)

✓ Decorative pillows

✓ Window coverings that help make your room more tranquil, and will close out sunlight if necessary

Bugs

No one wants bugs, mites, germs, bed bugs, urine or other fluids in their mattress. (I'm assuming no one does!) The worst deal-breaker is BED BUGS. It is possible they could be waiting for you in a used mattress, or any fabric furniture. They take over everything fast. You have to hire environmental pest control to rid your place of billions of tiny eggs and bugs. Not funny. Okay, enough of that.

Who makes the bed?

It is possible to make your bed daily. It's not like you have to do military folds and tucks. Pull up the covers, fluff the pillows, if possible, open the window (outrageous!) for a few minutes of fresh air. It takes one to two minutes, tops.

Some people say:

> I don't make my bed because I just mess it up again. That's like saying I don't change my underwear because it will just get dirty again.

You can spend a lot or a little to make a comfortable bedroom and place of retreat. What's the point? You do this for you. You deserve the welcome of a made-up bed, and clean sheets weekly. You. It's a personal kindness.

In the Closet

It is common to use the bedroom closet for sports equipment, stuffed animals, posters, computer boxes, large tools, vacuums, and empty hangers. It is common, but not necessary.

If you dare, you will be shocked at how much easier and faster it is to find and choose the clothes you want to wear from off a hanger on a rail. Clothing on the floor is always suspicious.

Don't worry, I don't think that you'll take this suggestion and run with it. It seems to be a rule that most people have to dig through piles of clothes for years, and some never find their closet or use it.

Just for the heck of it I will recommend stacking baskets in your closet for underwear, bras, socks, nightwear, and such. Nothing quite fits in the dresser, and you forget what you have in those drawers. The basket organizer means you don't have to fold these garments if you don't want to, except tee shirts.

These type of items segregate well into stackable clothing storage baskets:

Night shirts, pjs	Socks, white	Off season clothes
Shorts or panties	Socks, dark	Clean clothes you wear to do dirty jobs
Tee shirts	Bras and slips	
you might want them on a hanger—imagine	Workout clothes	

A closet organizing system will not hang up your clothes!

Mirror, Mirror, on the Wall

When you're out and about you will often be surprised at what some people are wearing. You wonder how they can walk out of the house looking like a pile of dirty laundry with chains and a hat. You wonder how those clothes acquired that odd set of mud-colors. The outfit might be completed with plastic garden shoes or bedroom slippers. It's just too easy to describe the many disastrous outfits or get-ups people wear in public.

We've all had our eyes hurt by the mutant pinky-gray stuff worn everywhere—and stretch-pants or huge pants. Just say, no. Look in the mirror before leaving home.

There's an old saying that covers the 'why' of checking one's self out before leaving; Golden saying:

You're behind it
You don't mind it
It's the folk out front
Who get the scare

If you want to fight ugly-clothes-syndrome put a full length mirror in the bedroom and/or by the front door. (They are quite inexpensive at the box stores.) This madness can be stopped at the door. Pause, look in the mirror. Do you want this vision burned in other people's brains?

Remorseless Rule

Murphy's Law of bad clothes: If you rush out of the house to buy something like milk, and cold medicine, and you're wearing the worst outfit ever— your bedroom slippers, and a hat/hoody to cover your hair—you will absolutely meet someone you want to impress.

They will run you down and you will be forced to stand and talk to them. It's miserable. It seems like hours and all dignity pass before you get away. This law is amazing in its consistency. It happens every single time.

To the hoodie and skirt-pants wearers, this is it! You don't get to do this again. You are in your prime. You have a full head of hair. You have energy. You may not think you're attractive, but with a little personal care, you are.

The forces of time and life, such as balding, weight, disease, wrinkles, and aging sneak up on everyone! Enjoy yourself now, before the arthritis and hair loss.

Time and Tide Wait for No Man
Or Woman

RESPECT the *Bathroom*

The bathroom is an all-important little room
that deserves your RESPECT!

Bathroom: a room containing a bathtub or shower
and usually a sink and toilet (in the USA).

I know, it's hard to focus when the topic is the bathroom. But
think about Second and Third-World Countries. What would
your life be like **without a bathroom?**

How would you like to share a bathroom with a dozen people
with no expectation of privacy. Think about sharing a toilet-
hole—not a toilet, a hole in the floor where wind will blow up
your skirts. And you'll wonder about what is in that air. Think
about places where you are not allowed to use toilet paper. Think
about not having running water, let alone warm water, let alone
a tub. Think about the smells.

Now, **thank the Lord** that you have a bathroom to clean. Be very grateful for plumbing, privacy, towels, and toilet paper.

It usually works out that of all your home-care purchases, the **plunger** will be the most beloved and useful of them all.

Cleanliness is Next to Godliness

The bathroom is a Petrie Dish. Flashback to Science Class. Do you remember those little round discs that contained gel medium for growing bacteria? You took a swab in the gym shower just for fun. Do you remember how fast the furry gray, green, pink, mystery stuff grew. Remember how you wanted to stop showering at school?

On the sliding scale of bathroom frequency-of-cleaning, or FOC, one can choose anywhere from 'never' to 'every day.' Once a week is probably a fair average unless there has been an emergency.

You want respect? If you know company is coming to your place, clean the toilet and sink. You can do it in three to five minutes. It can change your future.

> **Attractive and Hot Guest:** Can I use your bathroom?

> **Occupant:** Sure, it's right there.

> **Hot Guest goes in, comes right back out and says:** Oh, I guess I'll wait and use the restroom at the mini-mart.

Now, your entire life-hygiene will be in question. Your name has been entered onto the 'icky bathroom' list. (It not a list where you want to be included.) I repeat, you can change your life if you'll get out and move, and clean the bathroom.

Pick up your in-side-out underwear and dirty towels and other embarrassing things. If someone is staying overnight, spend another two to five minutes to clean the shower. Make it easy. Use a big brush.

For fun and sword practice, wield a brush in shower, **while you're in it**. A little preventative cleaning, spray, and brush will save you the angst and stigma of bathroom grunge.

Paper towel stand in the bathroom?

It may not be the look of a designer, but placing a roll of paper towels at your bathroom sink is a thoughtful thing to do. (You want to be thoughtful, right?)

Bathrooms are Suspicious

Put a small trash-basket nearby. Line it with a plastic grocery bag (recycle) so you don't have to touch anything when you remove it. EMPTY the basket at least once a week depending on the amount of traffic that goes through your bath. Never assume that your private bath won't be seen by others. It will. It's a law.

Applicable Law

Under Murphy's Law

Side Laws

If your bathroom is dirty, someone you want to impress will surprise you and ask to use it & visitors always clog the toilet; and...

Brooms are totally multi-purpose. In your bathtub or shower you can spray cleaner and the scrub it off with a clean broom and rinse that green goop down the drain. (There, that wasn't so hard!) It's fun to see the goop go down the drain. Remember, rinse the brush of the broom off in the sink or tub BEFORE and AFTER you use it so you don't pass icky stuff around.

Best way to do it: clean the bathroom, then take a shower. You're both clean.

Especially in warmer climates, your washcloth is sour after one use. A sour, sweat-sock smell means that germs are having a party. Do you want a sour face-cloth on your face? Do you remember what that means?

You might want to buy the big pack of wash cloths, and use a clean cloth every day. There are facial cleansing wipes if you can't handle the laundry and want a clear complexion.

Laundry Reminder: towels of all kinds are best washed in one separate load in the washer and dryer. Use bleach appropriately (read the directions).

Towel Warning: Towels washed with clothes will cause your clothes to have little white knots all over them, and it will look like you slept in your clothes on fleece sheets. If that's your look, carry on.

How Many?: At the minimal and efficient level, buy two to four bath towels, and alternate at least weekly. You'll also probably want a stack of wash cloths. (See hand towel warning.) In areas with high humidity, you may need to change towels more often. In areas where you decorate the floor and furniture with wet towels, you'd probably want get a dozen bath towels to start.

Decorating With Wet Towels: You may want to resist that urge to decorate your house with wet towels. No one and nothing is better for wearing a wet towel. If you cannot manage to get a towel over a bar, you can try to put up hooks and expend the super-effort to lift the towel upward and snag it on a hook. It's not as hard as it sounds.

Cute shower curtains: Now is the time to define your style. Yes, the bathroom is the easiest and least expensive room in the

house to decorate or make over. (Providing you're not changing out the big stuff.)

You can find any theme made for the bathroom from mathematic equations, to the tropics, to stripes, to bold modern, to maps, to flowers, to seashore, and more.

Look at you and your cool bathroom with coordinated shower curtain, towels, throw-rugs—and if you're all the way on board, you can also get a coordinated trash basket, toothbrush holder, and toilet brush holder. Okay, that's a little much.

Shower Gum: Back to reality, shower curtains get gummy with soap and skin residue and oils—and other stuff. Yes, you are oily. Yes, it is gross.

If you buy a fabulous exterior shower curtain, you'll want to splurge $2.99 and get a clear shower curtain liner. Then, when your shower curtain starts sticking to you, you can put in the washing machine on "cool" setting with a load of towels. After taking it from the washer, shake the curtain out, and re-hang it.

DO NOT put the plastic shower curtain in the dryer. The washed curtain will be wrinkled, but will straighten out with a warm shower.

Or buy a new lining for $2.99 and throw the old one away. If that $2.99 bothers you, some folk cut bottom off the curtain with scissors. Obviously, there will be a point when cutting is no longer a good option.

Oh, oh. **The wet floor law.** If you let water leak on the bathroom floor with any consistency, in any location, it will rot the floor. Rot and the accompanying mold and mildew is the worst word in property ownership. Tell the landlord right away. If he/she doesn't respond, leave another message. Now, it's on the landlord.

If you are living in a complex, and your water drips through the floor and pours out in your neighbor space below, he/she will be pounding on your door and screaming.

Respect the floor. That little bit of water on the floor every day does matter when it drips between tub and tile and vinyl. Mildew and soft wood problems need expert care and clean-up. You may even be enduring an allergy to mold, which is not good for anyone.

If you are smart enough to be a plumber or remodeler, your friends will soon cherish you.

Try not to be crazy. I know, it's hard.

Hi! New Friend?

Environment is all around you, and You are all around it

Law: Don't Mess With Nature

Safety tip: The natural environment has more power than we simple humans can comprehend. Even saying this is ridiculous. We are the grains of sand on the beach. So, if you get a storm evacuation notice, just go. This is not the time to try out the storm. Some of you will ignore all safety warnings, and stay and try and get some good photos. You are of an age to choose.

Environment: is a trigger word commonly used in our world today. In this case, we will look into having an environmentally sensitive home, foods, trash, and cleaning products.

I know, what you're thinking: *Caring for the environment is important, but I don't want to talk about it. They make me feel guilty way back to the times when I was in disposable diapers.*

Relax. We are only biting off environmental concerns in our **personal control**. If you want worldly environmental control, this book is not going to be helpful to you.

…and you will bring to ruin those ruining the earth.

REVELATION 11:18

Environment is a major topic for the pros, and you know where to find them. We're just swinging through the tops of the trees with the idea of hitting some obvious points.

Seriously—this topic deserves a library of its own, but you've been raised with most of the appropriate rules.

Sort the garbage as your location requires. You'll want to use environmentally sensitive garbage bags and take the garbage to its appropriate destination.

The top of the obvious list: Never dump your trash in the parks or wilderness or mountains or valleys.

Environmental Products

Consider whether you wish to buy or make environmentally sensitive cleaning products such as dish soap, laundry soap, bar soap, disinfectant, wipes, shampoo, oven cleaner, toilet cleaner, shower cleaner, trash bags—we could go on.

It has been rediscovered that cleaning with vinegar, soda, salt, lemon, (and so many other natural and effective cleaners) is regaining respect and a following. That kind of information is readily available on line, and they can present it with more accuracy, detail, and grace than I.

You might also want to check into environmentally sensitive food which is widely available.

I followed a woman through the check-out line; her basket was full. There was no meat, no junk food, no bread, no plastic—just veggies and fruits and cloth bags. You have to acknowledge the discipline it takes to buy and eat like that. Apparently it is possible, but I'd never seen it before.

Back to the grocery store, you have more choices to make. Food containers, baggies, wrap, napkins, paper towels, foil, baking paper, toothpicks, and plastic wrap for a few. Try not to buy too much.

Now we get into a sensitive area. Home.

Front porch dump

You will not be popular if you let holiday pumpkins rot on your doorsteps until summer. Your neighbors won't enjoy your dead, brown xmas tree in the yard. Recycle it. The neighborhood will be very unhappy if you stack up garbage, pop cans, plastic bottles, buckets, boxes, foam, dead flowers, cat litter, dog food, and the like on your deck or porch. And your friends will be afraid of what is inside.

If you're tempted to do that weird thing with trash, like putting it in the bedroom, crawl space, basement, hall, deck,

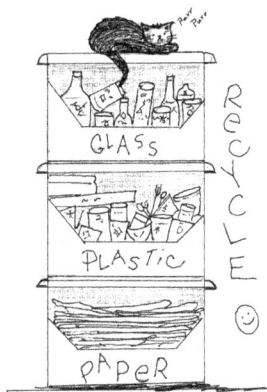

kitchen, or living room, think about it. Cat, mice, insects, squirrels, and larvae just love that environment. Then they die in the wall. The smell is evil, and doesn't go away for a long time.

FYI, that's called **hoarding!** You really don't want to see your family, neighbors, and a TV camera crew heading for your door. There are better ways to get your 15 minutes of fame.

If you live in the appropriate place, you can compost your food-trash. This works for people who raise gardens. But there are certain things that can poison a compost pile. If your inner naturalist is *calling to you,* look it up. Composting is very popular in gardening areas, and helps build up productive soil.

> **Compost:** a mixture that consists largely of decayed organic matter and is used for fertilizing and conditioning the land.

Environment, Sensitivity, Beasts, and Vermin

Keeping outdoor trash bins is not legal in many locations across the world. Why? Because the food smells attract dogs, bears, deer, raccoons, rats, insects and the like. It's generally safer and less expensive to see these animals in a book, or a zoo, or not at all in the case of insects. They are very destructive to property, and in some cases dangerous to humans.

Squirrels, mice, and rats are friendly, and they love plastic covered wires, and sheetrock, and can do an amazing amount of expensive damage digging around in the attic or walls. They have no wish to evacuate.

Raccoons are so darn cute, and they could be hired out as building demolition contractors. They also have a thing about plastic coating. When they move in, they are really, really hard to move out. Their kids and grandkids don't want to leave either.

Deer are so graceful and adorable, and they won't leave you a flower, berry, or vegetable. They can be very aggressive around their young. Those hooves are sharp.

Moose are such a wonderful conglomerate of parts. They can be the size of a camel. That's big, really big. They are not interested in being your pet. Their hoof print is the size of a pancake. They won't let you take pictures of their babies.

Bears are amazing to see, but not good to play with. In the search for food (preferably human food) they can and will tear down doors and walls, destroy cars, out buildings, and demolish super-lock trash containers. They are not afraid of you. And if you think a gun will protect you, I will remind you that there is only one place that you can put a bullet in a bear and hope to kill him. It's a small triangle in the chest, head on. Bears have double skulls so head shots don't count.

Other dangerous wild life who want your goods include insects. Miserable creatures, ticks, fleas, and mosquitoes carry dangerous diseases. Centipedes are just creepy beyond mention, and like a spider bite, they should send you directly to the doctor. A two inch roach with a hundred babies scooting around your floor will send the toughest of you to the top of a chair where you can't help it, you scream. Then you fall and hurt yourself. Screaming doesn't help. And, it's not okay to call the Fire Department or the Environmental Protection Agency.

In some warmer locales or apartment buildings they regularly spray for insects—but here you go with sensitivity to the environment again. You decide. It's your world.

Green, wet, and warm—vacation or nightmare

If you live in this environment, you will be happy and able to enjoy swimming and boating and gardening. You won't be happy if you leave a dirty dish in the sink overnight. You will get up to a train of ants stretching from the kitchen sink to the front door. (How do I know these things?!) Roaches like everybody. They'll happily take over your place. They don't pay rent, and they have no shame.

In warmer climates people also have a problem with bugs invading flour, cornmeal, sugar, cereals, rice and the like. If you don't want these bugs in your food, put everything edible in containers with lids, and don't leave crumbs and trash around. Containers run in price from reasonable to shocking, from recycled to new. But soon, you'll have your own home-grown containers as you consume food from plastic and glass containers. Jars that have been emptied and cleaned work well for see-through storage. Plastics without lids are almost useless.

I know, it sounds like a lot of work, but particularly in the warmer states where roaches are the size of a salmon, you'll need, no you'll want to keep it clean. This falls under the '**Risk-and-Reward' Law.** If you don't mind a two inch palmetto bug (roach) running over your head or arms as you sleep, you're tougher than I. You decide.

Furnishings, Rooms, Style, and Attitude

MID CENTURY MODERN

Furnishings: objects that increase comfort, necessary equipment, usually for the interior of a building... (At some point, cardboard boxes count as furnishings.)

Personal Germs: to be free of other people's germs; start with a clean place, it's a blank slate. Your own germs which, which will come, are preferable to others'

Clean it or not: few items out there that cannot be cleaned by one means or another; if you can't clean it you probably don't want it; be inventive.

The Critic's Club is alive and well, and competing with the World Police for first hit. For some tiresome reason, some people will feel free to critique or make unwelcome suggestions about your decor. Unless you want their input, you can tactfully remind them they get to furnish their place, and you get to do yours.

If you want help, find a person with similar décor ideas to yours, go treasure hunting, and have fun.

Take every comment about your place as a compliment. (This is actually a good rule for all walks of life.) It's your place.

If you want a wagon wheel coffee table that no one else wants, go for it. Some of the best, most fun pieces of furniture have been collected by people when no one else saw their promise. And, if you get tired of it, get rid of it.

If your idea of a restful room is a Spartan monk-like cell, do it.

Applicable Laws

Rule of Reality

Law of Right to Know

Law of Multiplication

Law of Germs

Law of Storage

and always
Murphy's Law

Take every comment as a compliment. You'll be so happy.

Don't look to the left or right,
And never compete. Never. Watching the other guy.
Is what kills all forms of energy.

NANCY COLLINS

You are not committed to keep everything in the same place after you move in. In fact, you probably won't quite like your first try. As you go, drag that furniture around and see if you can find a layout or look you like better.

If you've lived around family you probably have access to all kinds of furnishings. Most people have more stuff than they know what to do with. They're generally glad to share.

Please be careful with uttering words like: ugly, ick, horrible, hate it, eye rolls, and so on. Nothing shuts generosity down faster than the word ugly applied to someone else's things.

You might say something like: that's not quite the look I'm going for, but thank you for offering. You'll sound so mature.

Be kind. Don't bite the hand that feeds you. Ever.

Inhabit your home

If you go and buy all of your at furniture the same time, besides a pretty big bill, your place will look like a show room floor. If you're like most people, order will last up to a week. If that's what you've been dreaming of, and you have the money, there are so many great places to go for it. If you like eclectic mix, you can have a lot of fun searching out finds. Your furnishings should serve you and your senses: sight, smell, texture, color, and comfort.

> **Eclectic:** selecting what appears to be best in various doctrines, methods, or styles; composed of elements from various sources.

Places and Displaces

If you're renting a furnished room you can still make it yours. Fabrics can change the look of tables and chairs. Rugs can work on the hard floor or carpet. Small decorative rugs can be used as art. Pick great weaves, such as Indian, velvet, cotton, wool, and bamboo. Lamps, chairs, artwork, collections, bookcase, quilt or comforter, and good pillows can make at very small space livable.

Tough Looking Places

There are some rough looking rental spaces out there. You might have to live in one.

Take stock. If you can, take a little time. Use all your friend and family resources in difficult renting areas. You might find a place like an apartment over a nice garage, or mother-in-law apartment. Some people will rent rooms out, but they don't advertise. **Consider your list of rental deal breakers, and your list of must-haves.** You're going to have to put some time into this. And it still may not work out. That's called managing expectations.

A recent article in the newspaper by Lenny Bernstein was titled: **How housing affects your health.** (Look it up. It's tough out there.) Would-be renters will want to check for over-crowding, and adequate facilities for cooking, and bathing. I would add that your rental should not be infested with insects and vermin, and plan to avoid violent streets, and rooms over bars with bands will make you very unhappy. The ones of you **who don't have to worry** about this should be very grateful.

Look for potential. Can you fix this? Can you live here for a while? You may have to do a good scrub-down to see what you're working with.

Safety is its own major topic, which we have lightly touched upon here. However, this is a little, semi-serious book, not an encyclopedia. Safety is so subjective! It would be a good idea to **research your area specifically.**

A few no-brainers

✓ No key under the flower pot or on top of the door frame

✓ Secure your windows when you are not at home, and at night

✓ If you can, install or have a new lock, preferably a deadbolt lock and chain

✓ Your door should have a peep hole—if you don't know who it is, don't release the deadbolt—chains are only as secure as their installation

✓ Check smoke detectors to see if they work

✓ Make sure you have a fire extinguisher in the kitchen

✓ Pay attention to your parking area, consider carrying a demotivating spray or some protection —pay attention

✓ Consider a class on self-defense

✓ When you are not enjoying the sunshine, pull the blinds—check your windows from outside to see what others see—no peep show

✓ Night lights and motion lights, in the right space, can be safe and helpful, and inexpensive

✓ Know where all the exits from the building are in case of fire, earthquake, or storms

✓ Know your neighborhood and what is normal there

Dealing with the downsides:

If your window(s) provide terrible views like the alley, the garage, the dump, the highway, the mess next door, or the business across the street—the view can be mitigated. There are window sheers and window films with designs that go directly on the window that look like stained glass, lace, and other designs.

If you have a rotten deck view, that can be helped with a couple of potted trees.

If you take a basement apartment with gray walls, and you like light, paint! Use light colors and bright floor coverings. This is a good time to break out primary colors, and mid-century modern.

Call upon experienced family or friends to help fix and paint. Sometimes we genuinely don't know what we want by way of environment and furnishings. Don't panic. Cruise odd-ball stores and open houses. Hardware stores in small towns have a treasure trove of surprises.

A friend's parents bought him/her a new condo and furniture. Yours couldn't. Few can. Some would be swept away by this. Some would feel as if they missed something. This is not a contest. Character in an apartment, and charming location, is a way to experience another piece of life.

If you've never dipped a brush or roller in paint, or put a nozzle on a spray gun, it's time to earn your stripes. Find someone who knows what they're doing. Have fun. If you hate the color when you put it on, let it dry, and paint it another color while everything is still prepped. First ask the landlord!

52 Pickup

Our beliefs, thoughts, and **surroundings** have a powerful effect on the kind of person we are, and the moods we have. Try to **avoid depressing and angry home spaces**. You know what it looks like. You know what you feel like when you see it. Anyone who comes in your place will soon be depressed and demotivated too. When this happens, **stop**, and do a **52-pickup**.

There's a clever (not) game people used to try on younger people. They'd say: "Do you want to play 52 pickup?" The younger one would of course happily say: "Yes!" The trickster would pick up a deck of cards and spray them all over the room. (Hysterical, right?) "Okay, there's 52 cards, pick them up."

However, there is a home-health 52-pickup. Set the timer on 20 minutes. **Now go.** Pick up, throw out, and put back in place the many things that are cluttering your sight, your nose, and your brain. You'll be amazed how much you can do in a focused 20 minutes. The physical exercise, and making your mind up quickly, and being de-cluttered will make you feel better. I promise.

Time to play!

Now, are you ready for some ideas? There is so much stuff out there with great character. I've described a few home themes that will either be fun, or annoying. The annoyed are free to move on.

Steam Punk

You will either be intrigued, or terrify your friends and parents with this style. It leans toward funky antiques, junk-tiques, trunks, and dark rich colors, and velvets. Chairs, tables, and sculpture are made up of anything metal such as clocks, watches, phones, keys, tools, boxes, and machine parts. They are put together in fascinating detail. Top hats, coat and tails, gloves, mustaches, and eyeballs, are often part of the fabric, art, and clothing in this genre. Think of **Warehouse 13**.

Mid-Century Modern Design

Think middle of the last century, the 1950s. The design world was turned on its head. Think clean lines. No clutter. Primary color plastics. There was still a dial on the telephone, TV, and radio. Electric typewriters were not available to most people yet. (Ask your parents or grandparents.) Shag rugs, modern line chairs, straight-line flat couches, side tables the shape of a guitar pick are matched with giant ashtrays, TV trays, sputnik, and cocktail shakers, and torpedo and blimp shaped things. The animated show, **The Jetson's**, (ask your parents) had this style down. At the time people were looking forward to the space-age of flying cars, robot housekeepers, wrist phones, and instant fast-food at home. We keep looking.

See the **Roommate Agreement** on co-decorating. Nothing is permanent.

Later, if you hate something you may, give yourself permission to **get rid of it**. It's totally mentally and physically cleansing. Don't get hung up on perfection. It strangles creativity.

Buying All New Furniture

Can you afford it? Can you afford it on time payments? Because, a guy or gal still has to have a little in the budget for fun. The furniture stores often let you make **payments for five years**. It sounds pretty reasonable at the time. But you will be making 60—count them, sixty—payments. You decide.

Magazines and catalogues throw us all sorts of furnishing ideas. There are some you may not have thought of:

✓ Modern Basement Statement, dark or light

✓ Rich and Doting Parents Easy

✓ Motorcycle Modern Design with chrome, black and orange

✓ Bicycle as Art, and Creative Cardboard Mix

✓ Engineer Beige with the exciting new grays and metal furniture

✓ Computer Fanatic Design with furniture and art made from computer parts and metal

✓ Tattoo House Gothic, black, red, white and scary

✓ Lake Cabin Look, log tables, and end-tables, animal racks and driftwood, wool blankets

✓ Dry-land Nautical Style, maps, boat oars, life preserver, blue and white rope

✓ Upwardly Mobil Modern Box Stores

✓ Starving Artist, Writer, Actor, or Musician

✓ Medical School Messy

Sometimes you have to make something really ugly and get it out of your system.
Mess it up good, and throw it away. Start again.

GRETCHEN THOMPSON

✓ Fast Food Primary Colors Décor

✓ Inherited Family Composition Blend

✓ 350 Square Foot Efficiency

✓ Early Dorm Room Contemporary

✓ Garage Sale Composition

✓ Victorian Antique

✓ Nationality-centric Design

✓ White, Austere Minimalist Décor

✓ Black and White and Chrome Theme Décor

✓ Hollywood Mirror and Satin Theme Décor

✓ Your Own Eclectic Design

You can go crazy on the internet. There are great sites devoted to making you crazy, and sending out new ideas by the minute. You don't have to go there. Warning, if you do you will be hooked.

Storage The Good, the Bad, and the Ugly

Rule

Your stuff won't organize or store itself.

• •

Storage: Space or place for storing, the act of storing, the state of being stored, safekeeping of goods in a depository, electrical storage.

Stuff: materials, supplies, equipment, textiles, collections, clothes, art, camera, photos, electronics, appliances, paper, books, plastics, baskets, boxes, music, CDs, DVDs—office supplies, furniture, deco, bedroom, bathroom, and kitchen supplies—and so much more.

Chances are your living space will easily handle your stuff—at first. Then—as rooms and cupboards fill, ask yourself, will you control your stuff, or will it control you?

Do you want that organized closet package we see in ads? It's to die for, bedroom size, expensive, and you *still* have to hang up your clothing. One motivation to keep your closet well trained is the cost of the closet organizer. If that's what it takes…

For the most part, people suffer from too many clothes. Some still have outfits from high school, costumes, formal wear,—but mostly its jackets, tees-tees-tees, shirts, and jeans. The sentimental, collector, or gatherer makes most of his/her closet useless by keeping things that one doesn't wear. People often say they want a closet purge and makeover, but when push comes to shove, they don't have time or they can't part with their clothes. Even those with clothes and shoes that don't fit, and will never fit. That's only about 90% of us. Still, it's worth a try to go organized. It might stick. At least for a week.

We are pitched those organized-by-size pantries, and kitchen shelves without doors, or with glass doors. There are about ten minimalist people out there who will honestly keep them up. They're hyperactive and almost magical. If you're not Zen, if you're not high energy, you will soon have piles of plates, bowls, cups, and glasses everywhere. They will not look cute/handsome smeared across a shelf or counter. Still, for the look, many will have to try. I respect that. Keep on trying. We have to keep those stores in business.

We shouldn't forget all the things that are not for the closet. Those fantasy storage rooms are for a fabulous storage space with good light, movable shelves, and narrow isles, so everything is in sight. The truth is, a great deal of your storage demands will be empty boxes from various electronics: computers, TVs, games, and music—and their various storage bags with logos that we never use.

And then, there is sports equipment. This is what will most likely be in your closet because there is no place else to put it. If you're a sports dabbler, or semi-pro, it is *sports de rigor* to have all the pieces and parts. Bikes take about 8 different items of clothing without knee and elbow pads. Field sports, hockey, climbing, and training can each fill a huge military-size duffle bag. And, for the disciplined, that's not a bad idea. Then, if you have a garage, hang your equipment bags there. How realistic is that!?

You begin to consider off-site storage. Is there a place nearby? Is it open 24/7? Can you afford a couple hundred a month? Is it dry and temperature controlled? Will you remember you have things stored there? Is it more than a half-mile from your vehicle to your storage compartment? Will you go there? All good questions.

For those of you who are driven, or fancy free, the answer "no" to every question won't make any difference. You are determined to get a storage space.

Off-site Storage

Alarm! Think before you get an off-site storage space. Space rent of $120 a month (or more) adds up fast. Especially because the stuff you are storing is probably broken, or going out of date, or you'll forget you have it, or you won't like it anymore, or it's a 'someday' item, and someday never comes. Twelve months times $120 a month (which is low) equals $1,440 a year! Is your stuff even worth that much? Rent times two years is $2,880, and so on.

Storage Options:

Sports equipment, and bicycles: There are plenty of small-space –storage-options—racks, clips, shelves, hooks and more. Some of them are useful and artful. Some are not. You may hang your bike in your entry or hall and let it double as a form of metal sculpture, or the industrial look. You can use a big storage bench to hold the odds and ends. If you have more than one closet, you can devote that closet to equipment.

Internal doors are useful storage places. Clothing hooks, shoe organizers (not just for shoes), and craft and paper organizers can round up a lot of stuff and make it look orderly—therefore more useful when you need it.

If you're a smooth talker your parental units or friends might let you store your sports equipment, trophies, electronic boxes, or unneeded furniture in their garage.

Rule of Storage

You may not hold responsible the person(s) that make room for your storage items. If you have precious photos, collections, stuffed animals, special clothing, and the like, and you put them in that garage or basement—your things are at risk for water damage, mildew, bugs, and other shocking happenings.

I tried to contain myself, but I escaped.

J. Sue Smith

Imaginative Storage

Use your clever mind to check out your living areas. If you have no interest in storage, or how your place looks, skip to the next chapter.

Ladders, who knew? Wood or metal, folding and not-folding, ladders are versatile and cool. They can be used as towel racks, scarf racks, artwork racks, shoe racks, tool racks, magazine racks, and so much more. Make the ladder work for the theme of your place. Short folding ladders can be turned into side tables, two can be made into a large desk by using glass or a door as the top. Ladders with wider rungs can be used as rack for music discs, collectables, and books. Some like the shabby-chic vintage look of old ladders well-used. Some like the shiny aluminum. Some like paint spatters on the ladder. Have fun.

If your **landlord** doesn't want you to **paint** the walls, (be sure and ask!) you may be able to define your style by using space and colors and even the lines of a room with non-stick wallpaper, fabric, message boards, paint or art. These props can be moved or disposed of when you're ready for something new.

Collections can be corralled as art (for guys and gals) with glass containers, plastic containers, baskets and more. Containers can be found in most stores; hardware, crafting shops, and thrift stores. Glass container(s) work well for things you want to see. Gather your collection (beads, sea shells, jack knives, beach glass, pens, art implements, tools, keys, coins, rulers, marbles, ribbon, silver spoons, or whatever) and corral it in glass jars—big or small. See? Better.

Glass containers with lids can be a good place to store often-use cooking/baking items such as rice, oatmeal, nuts, tea, coffee, and sugar. If you wish, you can set them on the counter for convenience. (Remember the insects in the flour?)

An artsy collection of large-size books can be stacked next to a bed or a chair to act as a side table. If you want to fake an artsy book collection, go to garage sales and thrift stores who sell them very cheaply. Top the stack with a tray or game board.

The world of baskets out there offers every choice for storage and decor you can think of, and some you've never heard of. Metal, wood, woven, cloth, plastic, canvas, and so many more baskets can be used as a good way to group office supplies, pens, tool, nails, cooking utensils, or fruit. There are some great standing or hanging canvas bags at the hardware store—not your same-old bag.

Hardware stores are worth exploring. Especially if you like the industrial, cabin, or boat look. When a basket is really dirty and cheap, but has a good shape, wash it with soap and water and a brush, and let it dry. It will either survive, or it won't.

Perfection is about letting go.

B. SWAN

Getting Rid Of

The wise ones keep a box or bag in the clothes-closet and the hall closet. When something doesn't fit, it's not what you expected, it was a bad buy, or a gift that is not your style, set it aside for donation. Somebody wants it! When the box or bag is full drop it at your local thrift store.

Some (not all) areas allow people to put (decent) furniture and shelves on the curb as free for the taking. If you don't have a vehicle this can be a good solution for making room and moving things along.

There are magazines devoted to storage, and they're fun to peruse. If you like perusing (look it up).

Tips To Prevent Household Suffering

Keep your shoes on!

"Experience is a harsh instructor.
It gives the test first, then it teaches the lesson."

MARTHA LUNKEN

This is not supposed to be a book that gives ultimatums. Yet, there things that are could cost you medical, mentally, or mechanically. So, in that spirit, **please allow some dos and don'ts:**

Don't stick your hand in the garbage disposal. **Remember 'Final Destination.'** Fingers are important.

Don't pour grease down the drain!!! It never comes out well. Clogged pipes are a total pain, and expensive to fix.

Don't open a bottle with your teeth on a dare. You know it's stupid and it never comes out well.

I felt an obligation to slip this one in. **Don't** drink alcohol if there is the vaguest possibility you are **pregnant**. There are people who drink or use and have babies that will never be okay. I don't know how this is possible, but some women say: I didn't know that.

Don't use glass cleaner on your computer screens. (You knew that.)

Do check the wattage on your microwave and use it accordingly. It's not fun to have a coffee cup explode as you try to take it out of the microwave. (How do I know?)

Don't use melamine (hard plastic), untested pottery, or metal in your microwave. Talk about burnt fingers! (I have the feeling you have already tried that.)

Do learn how to use sharp knives with attention and care.

Don't chop vegetables while angry or while drinking alcohol. Seriously. A trip to the ER, six or eight hours of sitting around bleeding, getting shots, x-rays, and stitches, and paying for the pleasure is not all it's cracked up to be.

Do read the instructions and use the appropriate cleaners according to what you are cleaning.

NEVER mix bleach and ammonia when you are cleaning! It's like unleashing chemical weapons of mass destruction. Seriously, you can damage your lungs.

Don't put dish detergent in the dishwasher. The froth will roll uncontrollably around the dishwasher door and across the floor. Stop. Scoop the soapy water from the dishwasher into the sink.

Do buy a good **plunger** for your toilet. It's ugly and you **will** need it—at the worst possible time. (**Murphy's Law**)

You are having a get-together at your place, and Murphy guarantees, someone will stop-up the toilet. It's really gross, and embarrassing (everyone is pointing at someone else), and you **don't want to try** and fix that **without a plunger**. And it's kind-of expensive to call a plumber ($120/hour including drive time).

If the toilet is overflowing, **push up** the 'flush' handle. That will drop the tank seal, stop the water, and save you time on your knees in stuff.

Do pay attention to how loud you play your music or TV. You may have a neighbor you don't want to get to know. Seriously.

Do look at the expiration dates on your food. You know what could happen.

Do a check of your exits from the building in case of fire. *A real fire is evil, stupefying, and not at all funny.*

Do take out the trash regularly. You can do it in three minutes, a commercial. Remember the ants, mice, and roaches?

Do line your garbage/trash cans. Your trash receptacle should not be something that scares you.

Don't get pets, especially dogs, and birds, if you're not going to be home to take care of them and train them.

Animals are social, they need company and activity, and they get lonely and bored and no-kidding crazy. Can you hold your bladder 6 or 8 or 10 hours? Enjoy other people's pets and housesit until you're ready and have time.

Do clean the bathroom before visitors come. That or scare your friends off for life.

Do pick it up. If you drop it, splash it, or break it, clean it up in minutes now, or spend hours doing it later.

Foot and toe abuse

It's just not worth limping or needing a doctor's call for head-on contact with bar bells, boots, bowling ball, exercise equipment, suitcases, and big tools.

Dangerous toothpicks

If a person drops a toothpick on the floor the person behind him or her will ram the toothpick into their foot. If the toothpick has been used in one's mouth, the wounded *will* get a raging infection. You may need to see a doctor—for a toothpick…

Sneaky Cleaning

Back to the nuts and bolts of home care. You can do an amazing amount of picking-up in 10 minutes. Set the timer.

Phone cleaning

When on the phone you may wipe the counters, dust shelves, and put things away. Move things so they please your eyes more. As you're talking to Yolanda about her new swimsuits (which one looks best), walk through your place and pick up all the dirty clothes. Still talking, you may want to separate dirty clothes into loads.

You'll decide one swimsuit has to go back. Look what you've gotten done! And you helped Yolanda too!

You can do it. I recently heard a woman plan her friend's entire wedding while pushing a cart through the store. I don't think she missed a thing. However, her gray/brown bagged out sweats did undermine her authority a little bit.

TV, movie, reality show cleaning

A semi-interesting show is on and you feel kind of guilty for watching it. Grab a garbage sack and swing through the place tossing stuff while watching. It looks and smells better, right?

Fold clothes, dust shelves, or even make a meal (careful with the knives) while half-watching. Because it really doesn't take your whole brain.

It's not a bad idea to have a small screen in your bathroom and kitchen to distract you while you're doing the same-old-same-old.

Put a load in the washer, a load the dishwasher, or go through the mail.

You are burning calories, and missing commercials.

Guests on the Way and Overnight Company

Guests: Say your parents call to say they will be dropping by with a pie. Or, your potential-maybe called to say he/she will be dropping by with a little gift. Your co-worker freaks out, calls on his way to your house so you can fix his problem ASAP. The gang decides, last minute, that they will watch the game at your place. Your landlord is on his/her way over to pick up your rental check.

You need: *Emergency Quickie Clean!* Hang on, you've got 30-45 minutes to bring the place up to code.

Open a window or door for fresh air. Go through the whole place with a large trash bag and pick-up all the trash laying around, and that in trash containers. Take it out. Pick up your laundry basket and some wipes, go through your place, de-clutter, and wipe the table tops, and counters.

Put things back in drawers and cupboards. Put the dishes in the dishwasher. Put the laundry basket full of odds and ends in the tub and close the curtain. Close the bedroom and closet doors.

Last, grab the vacuum and hit every floor surface fast. Put the vacuum away. You did it!!!

Ding-Dong: If you have regular visitors, emergency rations would be helpful if kept on hand. It is polite to offer the visitor a drink, and at times snacks are appropriate. A pretty *safe* shopping list is: various cold and hot drinks, crackers or chips and cheese, and a pack of up-scale cookies. These will serve you pretty well for short visits. If dinner is called for, it's time to select a restaurant.

Overnight Company, Help!

Oh, great. You have overnight company coming. The place is a disaster. This is much like the quickie-clean, only this time it would be good if you had more time, and are fully committed. Also, this time the tub and refrigerator need to be cleaned too. Really. You now know the drill.

Put out clean wash cloths and towels in the kitchen and bathroom. Throw out the fuzzy things in the refrigerator. Wipe out the refrigerator, and the counter tops. Check the kitchen floor. Is it embarrassing? Vacuum or sweep and mop it up.

It is thoughtful to have a few groceries on hand. *As a minimum, have a half-gallon of milk, eggs, bread, peanut-butter, and jam.*

In the guest spot or bedroom, change the sheets on the guest bed. It's a good idea to lay a couple towels and wash cloths at the end of the bed. Have an extra blanket or comforter because some people get cold easily. Make room for the guest's bag, and have a lamp beside the bed. A clock and some tissues would be nice too.

You can try closing your bedroom and closet doors if your room looks like a thrift-store van just pulled up and dumped off its load in there. However, it's hard to sneak in and out of your room dozens of times, and you'll leave the door open anyway. You decide.

Take the time to look around and appreciate your cleaned-up place. It won't stay that way long with guests. It is the first impression that counts.

Now we venture in to the psychological side of housekeeping. Few can escape this malady.

The Woe of Chore Cloud

Chore cloud: having a great deal of work or errands or chores to do, but not doing them, thereby feeling guilty and raining on everyone's parade.

Do you have a *"chore cloud"* hanging over your head and dampening your mind? The cloud makes one look as if he/she is constantly anxious, out of focus, and being dripped upon.

If you hear yourself saying things like: my place is a mess, I'm so tired, I have too much to do, my schedule is so tight, I need to go on a diet, I'm working 12 hours a day, my car is in the shop, I have a thesis past due, my boss wants me to organize the filing system, I didn't have time to wash my hair, I don't have time to exercise, or, I have to do training exercises a minimum of 3 hours a day, the cat box is full, my floor is crunchy, no we can't meet at my place, I got a driving ticket for talking and driving, my roommate won't help clean, I still have moving boxes in my living room, I missed my fingernail appointment and my fingers feel awful, I can't find my coat/ bag/shoes/watch, I have messages backed up and people are getting mad at me, but I just signed up for a college class on line, and I'm expecting another baby, I'm putting on an anniversary dinner for my folks and I haven't started the invitations, I overran my bank account, and I'm starting my own jewelry business, and doing wedding photography on the side—woe is you.

You probably need a good therapist.

Almost every one of those clouds and wires above your head are initiated and maintained by you. Your choice. You are not alone. The present system of things has us convinced we need to run our lives at the threshold of hysteria. It's a trick.

We all have hefty to-do lists, want-to-do lists, and have-to-do lists. It's a disease.

You do have more control than you think. The words: "*no thank you,*" work just as well as the words: *"I'd love to."* Neither are wrong.

Remember, some people thrive on chaos. Think of President Clinton. Others prefer to fly under the radar. Think of President Ford.

Overcommitted? Carrying a chore cloud? It's up to you to decide if you must be over-committed. You have free will.

Plastic Packaging, Teeth, and Blood and Tools

Plastic-Wrapped: products (the stuff you buy and bring home), plastic food containers, plastic sealed jars of food, clothing tags, boxes, wrappers, foil, wire, cardboard, and titanium cord—all for our protection (not).

Organization: (this is helpful) being in the process of organizing; attempt to bring order to disorder.

Torture Tags: I know what you're thinking: after all we've been through, you have more bad news!

You bought it, you figure out how to remove the tags—hopefully bloodlessly.

Complaining doesn't help. No one will answer the phone, let alone a text or (what?) a letter. The people at the service counter will yawn. What can you do?

There was a time when fingers, a letter-opener, scissors, a small manual can opener, or a jackknife could serve you pretty well in all walks of life. As you know, that simpler and kinder time is gone.

Our world is vacuum packed, sealed, and welded.

Over the years the materials used for packaging have been—evolving. (Perhaps by themselves.)

Applicable Laws

Good Old Murphy is really comfortable in this scene

along with Law of Gravity

Law of Health

and Dental Insurance

Product armor, gummy tape, plastic labels, **safety closures**, unopenable food boxes and bags, security devices that leave holes in your garments, and jars stuck with labels are built to withstand Armageddon.

I don't know why.

You'll never eat undamaged food again if you don't have a pair or five of scissors, and metal snips, and a box cutter—all potentially dangerous tools. One of the most common reasons for an emergency room visits are for mangled fingers. (How do I know?)

Those wielding box-cutters need to take out extra emergency room insurance because we're all klutzes at the worst time. You cut yourself slicing onions and preparing a meal for friends. There is blood everywhere. Going to the emergency room takes most of the fun out of the occasion. But it is something to twitter about. And the bill will make you cry.

Ridiculous packaging is not going anywhere but to the dump, and you will not be alive by the time it becomes part of the natural environment. Don't blame me. Look it up!

As a result, you will need training for meditation and forgiveness.

And then there are bottle labels

Our bottled foods come with paperish labels that have been welded into the bottle or jar. Any effort to pull off the labels to recycle the bottles is met with insoluble glue that cannot be soaked, scrubbed, wire brushed, or cut off with a knife. What are they afraid of? That someone else is going to take their label? What in the world for? Would Granny pass their sauce off as her own?

Forgive me, but there are so many storage uses for glass jars that it is counter-environmental to fix it so the label and glue lasts longer than the jar. It isn't an accident.

Glass jars with lids

Staples can be stored against humidity and bugs. Bottles and jars can be used for canning or liqueur or wine or marbles or sugar or sweetener or candy. Some labels lift right off. Some don't. If you don't mind ribbons of permanent splotchy, tacky, dirt-gray glue and paper you're all set.

Plastic, Teeth, and Blood

Many people are predisposed to try and open, well, just about everything with their teeth. Commercial plastic is stronger than tank armor. Your teeth don't stand a chance. It's not a good idea to test your teeth anywhere but at the dentist.

Oddly enough, people enjoy seeing someone else break their teeth doing a trick.

Teeth versus metal, wood, plastic, rope, fists, bats, balls, pucks, and any number of other mistaken applications is risky and sick. Risky, in the long-term way it is risky to put your hand in a blender and let someone else man the switch. You might or might not get your hand back. You'll miss it.

There are so many things that can go wrong with teeth. And a person only gets **one permanent** set. No one is happy that they don't have teeth. It's hard to chew food without teeth. Teeth are part of our identity, and missing, chipped, or brown teeth—fairly or unfairly—say a lot about us, such as: I play sports without a mouth guard. I get punched in the mouth. I'm afraid of the dentist. I use my teeth instead of tools. And, of course there is fanciful: I open bottles with my teeth.

On top of that, infected and broken teeth are excruciatingly painful, and they don't grow back. *Try to keep most of your teeth until you die. Think about it.—I know, it hurts to think about teeth. That's why we have to.*

There hasn't been a resurgence of the need for false teeth for nothing. Go to the dentist. You've been warned, Bucky.

Don't mess with the teeth. It will only bring sorrow and infection.

Okay, I'll let that subject go and move on to another annoying manufacturer's law.

The **tag in your shirt** is rubbing and poking your neck. You put your hands behind your head and try to yank it out. You only succeed in strangling yourself and breaking a fingernail past the quick. There aren't any scissors in sight. You resort to teeth, but the thread these tags are sewn with is made with titanium. It feels like barb-wire. I don't know why. It's just a rule held up more strongly by the clothing business than the Constitution.

Tags are required to cut, scratch, and irritate the wearer—and be nearly impossible to remove without making a hole. If one takes a moment and stares at the tag imbedded in a piece of clothing, one has to make the leap to see it as deliberate on the manufacturers' part. It is fiberglass sewn to your shirt. Why? It might be a law.

Regardless, when confronting the tag, breathe deeply, pull off your shirt, and go find the good scissors. (A pack of scissors should be on your short to-buy list.) Get the scissors and go sit down in a place with good light. Use your scissors like a surgeon. If you tear or pull out a shirt tag it will leave a hole in your new shirt. And you can't take it back. Stores notice that kind of stuff. So do friends. "Got a hole in your new shirt, ha-ha-ha. Tried to cut out the tag, ha-ha-ha."

With the scissors you at least have a microbe's chance at getting the torture-tag-free without making a hole. It takes time when you don't have time. So you need needles and thread, or iron on fabric to do the repairs. Or we can pretend our shirt is supposed to have a hole there, and make some more.

For your sanity and inventory you will need a few **tools**. You may want them to look decent and convenient gathered up in a container. Physics tell us the container needs to be heavier than the things in it.

This is where you want to be friends with someone in Pottery 101. Think heavy bottom. You compliment the artist and ask if they will part with their bottom-heavy pots that they made in class. These are the best counter-top tool holders. You could put a ski in the container and it wouldn't tip.

When gathering tools it's a good idea to add a letter opener, scissors, fingernail clippers and files, a screwdriver, and tin snips—even a small hammer. Next to that, you will want to have a container for pens, pencils, markers, and colored pens.—That or you can make yourself crazy looking for this stuff in various junk drawers, or under the furniture. Your choice.

You will at some point need each of these tools daily. If you can get to your tools before you have a fight with the tag or bag, you may be able to open the package without holes or blood. No promises.

Good idea tools:

✓ Bottom-heavy containers for tools

✓ Scissors

✓ Screwdriver

✓ Tin snips

✓ Hammer

✓ Fingernail clippers and file

✓ Ruler

✓ Pens

✓ Pencils

✓ Thread and needles

In case of emergency notify _____

You're never too old to do something stupid.

Manner-isms

*It's not all about you, or you rarely get
a second chance to prove yourself*

Frequent Word!

You're out on your own and running with the big kids. Embarrassing yourself is probably not high on your list. Manners at various events reveal one's character and maturity. People do notice.

Out to Dinner

Someone else is paying. It's a good idea to put your napkin in your lap. Try not to act like you won the lottery when someone else is picking up the tab. Ask the 'payer' what he/she is having a stay in that price range. Follow their lead on drinks, alcohol, side dishes, and dessert.

The Device Test

Do you join the conversation or do you spend the time looking at your lap and scrolling your device? With your friends you'll

> "We never really grow up, we only learn how to act in public."
>
> FROM INTERNET

be device centered. In formal or professional situations it's best to leave the device in the pocket.

If you don't like what you are served, find something you can eat on the plate or in the bread basket.

The dining debate goes on

Much of the food served at restaurants and parties hits at the 'okay' level. Complaining and picking at your food and arguing with the waiter is off-putting. You can choose to buck up and let others enjoy their food. Or not.

Other tips that apply—male and female: Think.

Open and hold the door open for others. As you know, it's not fun to have those heavy doors close on your hands or face.

It's just polite. When an older adult is standing for some time, and there are not enough seats, offer him/her your seat.

It is appreciated if you use your indoor cellphone manners. Talking louder really doesn't help.

A while back, as I cruised the grocery store, I passed this adviser-cell-phone-guy on every isle. He was giving another guy instructions about his divorce—word-for-word what he should say and do. I'm sure it didn't come out well.

Keyboard Commitment

Anything that you commit the keyboard can and will be *shared with the universe!* This warning is incredibly important, but it will not get the attention it deserves. When your information goes to the wrong place, the ground won't be so kind as to open up and swallow you, no matter how hard you pray. You can't put the genie back in the bottle.

"Offend-you!"

Some people think they have a way with words. If you are one of these people, take a look at the faces around as you're are holding forth in a conversation. If you see people wincing, blinking, and red-faced, *because of what you're saying*, it's time to reconsider your choice of expressions. You have *f-rash*.

Swearing, where the f-bomb seems to be a quarter of one's vocabulary, sounds emotional, like a flailing, out-of-control drama-queen or drama-king. The repeated use of the same word shows a narrow range of vocabulary. If that's the identity you're going for, you got it. *Skip to the next chapter.*

Request

Please try to control your f-rash when around work, family, children, and elders. There's only one group where this language is honored. Otherwise, it's embarrassing to you, and you won't know it until later.

Many people do not know this, but swearing is communicable. In some places it spreads quickly. Many people will catch that rash at one time or another in their life. Sadly, some people keep their rash for life, and it is often accompanied by a beer-rash.

Recently, in traffic, a young woman sent me an f-bomb and a pumped fist. Then she realized she had prematurely used her f-energy. It was embarrassing for her. It's hard to do this right, especially since the f-*word* doesn't mean anything more than "offend-you".

Personal Creed Indeed

Personal Credo: A set of fundamental beliefs, personal guidelines, or religious beliefs; from the Greek words *I believe.*

Everyone has their own personal set of **Laws and Rules**. Some just don't know it yet.

Ask yourself, who am I? Where is my inner compass?

I know. I've asked you to think too much for too long. It's hard enough to keep up with your electronics as it is. Now you need to fit in a space for a personal credo!?

Well, you don't have to do it right now, but it is worth considering.

Your personal creed

It's useful to write it down. Since you probably don't know you have a credo, it could be interesting to find out what your credo is.

Draw some lines, on paper/tablet and in your mind, as to what you will and will not do. You'll find yourself fascinated by yourself. *You* really didn't know *you* at all.

So, what's it all about?

The following are suggestions and good things to toss about in your head, kind of like salad.

You *will* find yourself making *yes, no,* and *maybe* decisions on *every* topic that follows. And not necessarily in any order. You can see how considering this list might help you to know who you are, what you'll do, and what you won't do. I must repeat:

Applicable Laws

Murphy's Law

Law of Diminished Return

Law of Right to Know

Law of Attraction

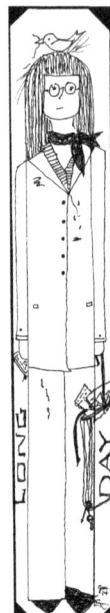

> "If you don't stand for something, you'll fall for anything."
>
> WISE SAYING

> "Calm your mind... No problem can be solved by a drunken monkey."
>
> E. A. McCULLY

What are you okay with, or not okay with?

- ✓ How far will you be pushed?
- ✓ Dating
- ✓ Marriage
- ✓ Sex
- ✓ Family
- ✓ Employment
- ✓ Money
- ✓ Honesty
- ✓ Friendship
- ✓ Religion
- ✓ Drugs/alcohol
- ✓ Generosity
- ✓ Entertainment
- ✓ Manners

- ✓ Ambition
- ✓ Introvert/Extrovert
- ✓ Education direction
- ✓ Work in the crafts (plumbing, electrical, heavy equipment, building, etc.)
- ✓ Responsibility
- ✓ Who are you? WHO? WHO? WHO? WHO?
- ✓ How do you feel about fitting in
- ✓ Do you like to do things by hand
- ✓ How do you react to anger or fear

- ✓ Stress (then add college and job to the columns as appropriate)
- ✓ What is your personal cleanliness scale
- ✓ What are your vulnerable areas
- ✓ What are your personal strengths
- ✓ What is ok/not ok in friendship
- ✓ Do you prefer being surprised or prepared
- ✓ How important are hair styles, clothes, and tattoos
- ✓ Where in the world do you want to live

I know! It's crazy. And I could add a hundred more! But I won't. And no one will ever know if you wish to mine your mind, or if you run screaming into the night saying: I don't want to do this!

Freedom. Your choice. If you **are** spooled up to check yourself out, I don't recommend that you try and do it in one day.

Murphy's Law will pop up on you whether you're ready or not. It comes down to: do you like the excitement of being blindsided, or do you prefer to be moderately prepared?

Thus, we have the famous sayings of the unprepared:

✓ I had no idea!

✓ I hadn't thought about it! I didn't expect it but I love it! I didn't know what to say!

✓ I didn't think it meant that!

✓ That scared the snot out of me!

✓ Will that tank my credit?

✓ I shouldn't have been there!

✓ I didn't know what I was getting into!

✓ I can't believe I got caught up in that!

✓ That was crazy—do it again!

✓ That cost me a fortune!

✓ Call 911!

✓ Will that be on my permanent record?

✓ I realized I don't like to do that, and I never want to do it again!

✓ Don't call my parental units!

✓ Don't tell my boss!

I'm sorry to share this news, but you're in the hysterical years. That age comes in the years from teens through twenty. It is an intense time. You're so invested in going forward. Some people know what they want and dive-bomb into it. Others wait for a clue, a clear direction from above, divine or not. You will treasure some memories and be haunted by others. Worse is not trying.

There is no *erase* button in life.
There is, however, a time to put the past to rest.
The *past being passed* is one of the strictest of laws of nature:
You can pray all you want, but you cannot go back.

J McCart

Me, Myself, and I

You don't have to write a book about yourself unless you want to. You can narrow-down the questions to those that draw your attention right now.

Gut Trusting, Heart Trusting, Pro and Con

Can you always trust yourself? Probably not. Since the beginning of time, most of us have had **two minds warring** in our heads. They used to be characterized as the *angel* and the *devil* posted on each shoulder. When *they* argue, you're in trouble. It's like there are two of you: one emphatic **"go"**, the other emphatic **"no"**. You watch yourself and are truly surprised to see which one of you wins, and what comes out of your mouth. We're complicated.

> I didn't say it was your fault. I said I was blaming you.
>
> INTERNET

It is popular to say: *trust your gut*. Or, *go with your heart*. Some pretty **bad decisions** have been made when depending on one's excitable gut for good advice. There is always a terrible idea you cannot resist, you know you'll be sorry, but you are sucked in like a leaf in a vacuum. It's a Rule. (See *Bridezilla, and House-wives*.) This is all part of the "*regret and rejoice*" years. No one goes through it without some breaks and bruises, and hopefully some laughing good times.

Information Cloud

Chores can be done. Information cannot ever be done or undone—unless the world has an electronic melt-down.

J. McCart

In the previous century, people were more careful with their personal information. There was a little more dignity in privacy. Now we all have an **information cloud** that carries our personal information beyond any place we will ever visit. Although it doesn't look it, the *information cloud* is much heavier than the *chore cloud*. It is also more vulnerable.

Personal privacy has a lot to recommend itself. Read spy books and think like an **international spy**. What information could hurt you? What do others need to know about you? What do you want others to *know* about you? What do you want to know? Where is your control of your personal information? Do you have a secret stash for emergencies? Do you prefer being wild or careful with your information, or off the grid?

No one wants to be type-cast. However, there are some definite categories of personality out there. It helps to consider that as you move through the maze of life. There is a personality test that offers these types:

- ✓ **Expressive people** love attention and will let it all hang out. Often too much.

- ✓ **Driver people** want to get the job done with minimum fuss. Sometimes they knock people out of the way on their quest.

- ✓ **Amiable people** want to make everyone happy. They can't. But they always try.

- ✓ **Analytical people** want every single bit of data, available or not. So they can get very hung up in the details.

Unfortunately, we are who we are. Fortunately, we are who we are. This gives us a little material to work with when relationships get confusing.

Still, no one needs to add screw-up photos, and angry rants, credit problems, and work problems to his or her life information cloud.

There used to be a saying: **it really is no one's business**. You don't hear that very often anymore.

It's out there—in the Information Cloud—and contains more than we dreamed. There's nowhere to run, nowhere to hide. But you can keep a lower profile.

Money

Money Makes the World Go Around, the
World Go Around, the World Go Around

SONG FROM MUSICAL CABARET

Law of Money

It will never be enough, it will never be fair, you only
think it is.

● ●

Money: something generally accepted as a
medium of exchange, measure of value, or means
of payment; wealth that is reckoned in terms of
money; it's something to fight about; it's
something to need or want; it always costs more
than it's worth.

To: Financial advisors, bankers, accountants, stock brokers, and sticklers everywhere

If you're out there, this is **not** the book for you. This is a friendly overview for those newly on-their-own, not a thesis for a lifetime investment program. In case you feel the need to comment, you should know that I will have a depressed person in charge of my messages.

I lived through the banking of the past 20 years. So, I **do** know how you feel. I know that talking about budgets and money and savings and minimum wages and too few jobs and retirement and insurance does make one feel as if they are smothering in hair gel. It's further depressing to realize that our famous 1% population of super-wealth seem to be the only ones who know how to work it.

There are no coincidences with money.

J McCart

But, the **Laws of the Universe** dictate that you will be exposed to money, and you will have to manage your financial expectations. It's so depressing, and yet so necessary.

Money is tricky.

Especially since the better part of it is on one card or another, one computer or another, and rarely cash. Hard cash is still there for the discreet, the debtor, or lawless. But, for how long? Every day the news tells us that security and privacy are a thing of the past. Minimum wage? Stock market lotto? Will *bitcoins* take? Then what? Will banks make it impossible to buy a house? What about offshore accounts?

It makes one nostalgic for the proverbial *pink piggy bank*, or money under the mattress. It offers about the same interest on your savings as the bank does. All of this makes losing track of spending so head-spinning easy.

> I used to be indecisive. Now I'm not sure.
>
> J. SUE SMITH

Money is not fair

It's never enough. It always spends faster than it gathers. It's easy to borrow at the payday loan places. It's easy to build a bad credit report. This can lead to moving back home, which will make you feel as low as a sell-slip on the stock market floor.

Personal Law of Borrowing Money: Money is never free.

You can easily go into debt and buy a whole lot of totally great totally necessary stuff right off the bat: electronics, appliances, clothes, collectables, furniture, vehicles, vacations, and so much more. Many sales programs give you up to five years to pay. That is 60 months. You aren't much older than 60 months! Think. Sixty payments. How old will you be? How old will your stuff be? How can you plan that far ahead?

Applicable Laws

Law of Diminished Return

Law of Gravity in the stock market

Law of Unintended Consequences

Wise Words

There is no such thing as a free lunch, cheap money, or easy money. For your own good, please tattoo this on your brain.

Going to 'quickie' lenders sounds good for 30 seconds. They have persuasive, professional commercials. It sounds too good to be true. It is. Un-friend them.

Going to certified banking lenders is also embarrassing. They will make you feel as if you should bow and stick your little pinky finger out as you sip the water you brought because your mouth is dry, and they are cutting back on water. If you need money, you are in need. You have no power.

But, respect yourself and respect the way you handle your finances. Savings get respect. Every day in the 'rejoice and regret' years will offer you opportunities to second-guess yourself financially, career wise, relationship wise—be aware.

It looks like the USA is now converted mostly to a service industry provider, rather than being a more lucrative manufacturer-producer as it used to be. What does that mean? It means our world has changed a great deal in the last ten years.

It means that a higher number of the jobs out there are in service industries, and they pay lower wages. It makes some college degrees no more helpful in getting a job than high school diploma or a café menu. Don't despair, unless you want to. The crafts (plumbing, electrical, heavy equipment, building) and electronics are still alive and well. Current logic says those jobs should be there for a while. No promises. And, there is always gold mining.

What does this mean to you? It means, GAME ON. It means being creative and thoughtful. It also calls for a firm personal credo and personal discretion.

game on y!

Price of Freedom

So, have you thought about what freedom is going to cost you? The saying: *Freedom isn't free,* applies to more than military service. What's it going cost you to be out there on your own? These are some of the various payments you can expect:

Wise words:

It's not a good idea to discuss your personal finances with other people in your personal life.

✓ Rent or house payment, rent or house repairs and maintenance

✓ Car payments, car maintenance (tires, oil change, new radiator) and car insurance

✓ Bus or subway or toll road fees

✓ Electronics: Internet/phone/ tablet *and* upgrades, *and* the next new phone/tablet you can't resist

✓ Medical and dental insurance and deductibles

✓ Utilities: gas, electric, oil, trash, water

✓ Clothes

✓ Groceries and cleaning products

✓ Dining out

✓ Entertainment

✓ Credit card payments

✓ Coffee Drinks

✓ Partying

✓ Cosmetics

✓ Hair and nails

✓ Church

✓ Lessons

✓ Books and music

✓ Sky diving

✓ Mountain climbing

✓ Designer anything

A little scary...

Unfortunately one needs to put the old brain in gear about now. How much income do you need to pay your bills? How much income do you need to cover the other stuff?

There is a calculating rule of thumb you may wish to use. It's not perfect, but it is more accurate than some would believe. At my big box store, I add up the number of items in my cart, and take that number times $10. I always come out within $5 of my estimate. Remember, an unusual buy can blow that theory to pieces.

Now, just for average sake, we'll take $100 times the number of household expense items we noted earlier, say 18. This is a very low/soft estimate. We are looking at this *just to get you thinking vaguely about real costs.*

Say we take $100 x 18 of the various payments listed. That equals $1800 in bills monthly, give or take. Minimum.

So, then, how much do you have to make to keep your head above water?

Also consider: Say you work 40 hour weeks, and then pay taxes, take out about 25% or more that depending on where you live.

You would be having a stressful time keeping your head above water with a wage of $16 to $18 an hour, working **full** time.

This does **not include** the common possibilities of having your work hours cut, needing extra time off, using up your savings, getting married, going to college, having a baby, having your car give up the ghost while you're still making payments, emergency flights, having a family crisis or death, and/or any other unplanned situations and bills.

> "Calm your hair down."
>
> J.S. SMITH

Not listed in the 18: vacations, gifts, household upgrades, long-term illness—let alone the latest coffee maker.

If your parents don't own houses, yachts, an island, a wine cellar, jewels, famous pieces of art, priceless antiques, a state of the art security system and the like, they are not in the 1% of wealthy Americans. So you're not either.

Many qualified folk are being **involuntarily retired**, or are unable to find a job when they hit their 50s and up. Their once reliable income is no longer reliable. It's happening every day. It means your parental units may not be able to help you out with money if it comes to that.

Work?

There is a lot of inspired *personal downsizing* going on, along with corporate downsizing. Now we know that financial **anxiety will always be there**.

At this time it seems a good idea to be brought up and educated in the crafts: pipefitting, electrician, heavy equipment, telecommunications, trucking, builders big and small, electronics, engineers, procurement, and more. These are probably the safest (?) group of jobs that pay nicely.

It follows that small, home based businesses may become more popular. There doesn't seem to be anything such as a stable job. Remember, income from home businesses is inconsistent.

So, what can you do?

There are inventive trends picking up on deep pockets of Gen X. Pets (because they are so much sweeter than most people) are taking a remarkable bite of the business pie.

People are actively designing and building very small homes which have an appeal. Further, these may be the only homes most people can afford to buy in the future. It appeals to those seeking simplicity.

Major **publishing** houses got so they chose only safe, re-published fiction authors. It follows that there are only a very few well paid authors out there, and a *lot* of unpaid writers. That was yesterday. The net is changing all that. Topics of interest, expertise, commentary, and fiction and nonfiction stories are being sought and published on line. There is now wiggle-room for writers of *all* subjects to earn a little money.

Arts, crafts, jewelry, antiques, purses, and clothing all have a resale place. Generally the satisfaction is high, but the profit is subjective.

Photography and film are going to all new places with the continual growth of the ton of reality shows, channels, and youth sports that are being broadcast. Photographic education, and experience actually means people can make a living with a camera.

It's against the law for a person to ride a bike wearing anything less that the outfit and gear of *The Tour DeFrance*. It is a law, isn't it? There's room to grow in specialized sports accessories.

No sports people have just one snow board, one set of skis, one hockey stick, one bat, one mitt… you can take it from there. Sports and camping gear providers keep designing newer and better and warmer and lighter stuff. It seems encouraging.

Concussion sports have opened the opportunity to develop a helmet for the full gamut of sports, recreation, work, space, theme parks, basket-ball and bowling. *Curling* is getting a whole new following since the Olympics. And those curlers' shoes and brooms and stones are not cheap. *Shark Tank*, here you come!

There is opportunity—just not the type of opportunity that was common in the past. Chain stores allow you to wonder if you ever left home (offering transferrable skills, if not big wages), be that in Hawaii, Alaska, Florida, Ohio—(don't make me list all the states and countries).

The micro-brewers and chefs and those making specialty treats are having fun and making a little money.

There are a lot of people working at banks, by far the most of them live on fairly unimpressive salaries. It is a good transferrable skill. If you're into big money, investments, and stocks, you pretty much need to marry into the family.

Baby Boomers, Gen X, Y2k, and the other generations are moving into a world of different spending priorities as they age. Hearing aids are coming on strong, as are glasses. Joint replacement surgery is becoming common. Senior care is already bursting at the seams—here comes the Baby Boom. Will there be opportunities to provide service to those who just don't do computers? Yes, there are people who just don't want the computer. They weren't raised to it, and got washed down the tube in rapid electronic changes.

Managing your costs and savings is a personal challenge. If you can master a computer game, you can hope to manage your finances. Be creative, keep your eyes wide open. There is opportunity in downturns—in unfilled holes left in the wreckage of the producer based economy.

Working folk will have to be creative, and sometimes fearless. But doing that can meaningfully alter the cost of living, and the way we're living. Less can be more. Be ingenious.

We can't expect to go back to money as we knew it in the 20th Century. Those fields have been plowed under. Life will only let us go forward, not back.

Be different.
Less is more.

Accidental Education

Every now and then we need
to eat all the cookies we want.

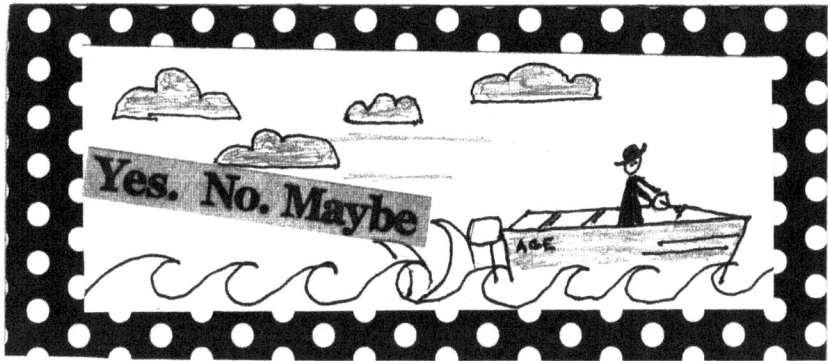

You can make your own education and your own base camp. Your own place. Now you have a general idea of how take care of your home. There are so many things that are not in this book. So many things that you won't expect. Yet, you can take refuge in the rule that says **There is nothing new under the sun.** No crises, governments, wars, finances, religions, or developments, that don't go down well-trodden historic paths. We're all in the same soup.

Millions of others will make many of the same *discoveries* and *mistakes* that you will. You're not alone. There will be enough anxieties for every day, as there always has been. When you grasp that knowledge, you're not fighting up-hill and clueless.

Time flies whether
you're having fun
or not.

Someday you will find tropical fish and coral reefs incredibly fascinating. You will actually chose to do laundry and be happy that you didn't go to that party. You might even start *bowling* or *curling*. This time line is coming at you faster than you could ever imagine.

LIVE NOW suggests that it is a good idea to develop your own credo in the face of flying time. Even if you're not friendly with the Bible, history, or the many other learning manuals, your brain might enjoy seeing where these wise and surprising adages come from.

It's amazing how these truths, laws, and rules have held fast over thousands of years. Be curious, look it up.

You're free, you're free, you're free! Now what? History repeats itself, and so do I.

Fear in the Cloud and on Earth

Nothing major has moved forward in the USA in the last twenty years due to various interests belting out comments and opposition—on just about everything, for just about every political reason. Call them the world police, the critic's union, or the big *they*.

We live in a time where within seconds we can be nationally mischaracterized, threatened, or called a fool for putting our toe in the water, or the cloud. We also live in a time when it's probable that everyone will have their 15 minutes of fame, good or bad. This goes to support the theory: the bigger they are, the harder they fall.

The dark side of life experiences and critiques is that they can discourage good ideas

> "So let us pursue the things making for peace, and the things that build one another up."
>
> ROMANS

or plans. It helps if you can recognize it for what it is: *life discouragement*, or **life support**. Take back your courage from the *discouragers*.

> **Dis-courage:** Allow someone or something to take away your courage; to make you less optimistic, and to make somebody feel less motivated, or confident, or optimistic; try to stop someone's actions.

I've enlisted the help of a friend who is a "spy" and will review all comments and delete the angry, threatening, and spurious comments that accidentally find their way to me.

After that, I will activate the rule of: *every comment about the book is a compliment.*

It is never wrong to be kind or gentle. You will be tested.

This is powerful advice, and a positive concept that will test you and turn out to be for the best. Now go and read about the Roman Empire. You'll be amazed.

You can't keep learning at this rate or you'll be really smart.

• Me & ROSE·MOLLY·Tessa

It is a law that if one writes a book, then one must write a bio. It is probably the least read page in the book. This is where one might measure themselves by listing degrees, impressive jobs, good investments, and famous friends. I can't remember that stuff, but I'm not sure it turned out well. So, now what?

To: My Husband, Dick. Thank you.

www.ingramcontent.com/pod-product-compliance
Lightning Source LLC
Chambersburg PA
CBHW060831050426

42453CB00008B/651